Other Titles from National Baseball Hall of Fame Books

Picturing America's Pastime:
Historic Photography from the Baseball Hall of Fame Archives
2021

Memories from the Microphone: A Century of Baseball Broadcasting
2021

SO YOU THINK YOU KNOW BASEBALL

SO YOU THINK YOU KNOW BASEBALL

The Baseball Hall of Fame Trivia Book

Cover Design: Elina Diaz
Cover Photo/illustration: Milo Stewart Jr. / National Baseball Hall of Fame and
Museum
Layout & Design: Elina Diaz

All statistics used in this book were sourced from Baseball-Reference.com,
which in 2021 began listing Major Negro Leagues (1920-1948) with the
American League and National League as major leagues.

For permission requests, please contact the publisher at:
Mango Publishing Group
2850 S Douglas Road, 2nd Floor
Coral Gables, FL 33134 USA
info@mango.bz

For special orders, quantity sales, course adoptions and corporate sales, please
email the publisher at sales@mango.bz. For trade and wholesale sales, please
contact Ingram Publisher Services at customer.service@ingramcontent.com or
+1.800.509.4887.

So You Think You Know Baseball: The Baseball Hall of Fame Trivia Book

Library of Congress Cataloging-in-Publication number: 2021944398
ISBN: (print) 978-1-64250-769-0, (ebook) 978-1-64250-770-6
BISAC category code: SPO003030, SPORTS & RECREATION/Baseball/ History

Printed in the United States of America

The crowd outside the Baseball Hall of Fame for the first Induction Ceremony in 1939.

Table of Contents

Artifacts from the Museum's collection, including some related to baseball's centennial celebration in Cooperstown in 1939.

Photo credit: Milo Stewart Jr./National Baseball Hall of Fame and Museum

Introduction

It was the early 1980s—the heyday of AM radio call-in talk shows.

The young student frantically dialed the rotary phone, sure they had the answer to the baseball trivia question just posed by another caller. Following the rules of the game, anyone correctly answering a question then stayed on the line with another query until it was successfully identified.

When the correct answer was given, the new caller offered what was thought to be the World's Greatest Baseball Trivia Question:

> Who was Eddie Gaedel, the three-foot, seven-inch batter for the St. Louis Browns, *pinch hitting for* on Aug. 19, 1951?

Surely, in a time when the internet was barely alive, no one could answer this.

Three guesses later, Browns' outfielder Frank Saucier's name was announced as the correct answer and the new king of the knowledge mountain was crowned—proving once again that someone, somewhere knows the answer to every possible question.

For more than 150 years, the National Pastime has compiled facts, statistics, records, and numbers in an organized fashion. This data has allowed fans to compare and contrast players of different eras, generating endless debate and passion. And for those so inclined, the details allow the opportunity to show off their knowledge through an infinite variety of questions and answers.

The library at the National Baseball Hall of Fame and Museum is where that information is forever preserved. More than three million documents comprise the stacks in and beyond the Giamatti Research Center, including player files on each of the 23,000+ batters and pitchers in big league history.

Magazines, newspapers, media guides and even day-by-day records for the leagues hold secrets untold—their answers waiting only for a researcher's eye. Then there are the compilations—"Total Baseball," "The Baseball Encyclopedia," and the brilliant Neft & Cohen series—each of which could supply knowledge for a lifetime.

Then, the internet made that knowledge even easier to access and correlate.

If you love baseball information, our library is your Valhalla.

Our library team calls this their home—and are asked daily to access it all. They may not have every answer memorized, but they have the perfect response when stumped.

"We may not know the answer to every question," the librarians say. "But we know where to find the answer."

No other sport reveres its history like baseball. It's the unbreakable thread that connects Ty Cobb to Mike Trout, Roberto Clemente to Ronald Acuña Jr., and Hank Aaron to Mookie Betts.

With the present always summoning the past, the game becomes a circle of respect. And fans pay their respects through gaining knowledge of the past and sharing that knowledge with one another.

And the best part? Trivia questions are really fun.

So You Think You Know Baseball is meant to challenge the most serious trivia fans with insightful questions based on the game's endless connections. You'll turn each page and say "I never knew that"—feeling history come alive through the decades.

And when you get to the final answer, you'll be ready to challenge your family and friends with some of the most amazing and eye-opening trivia in the game's history.

No matter your baseball IQ, *So You Think You Know Baseball* promises to bring home the winning run in your trivial pursuit.

Chapter 1

Baseball Firsts

"If I had one wish in the world today, it could be that Jackie Robinson would be here to see this happen."

—Frank Robinson at his introductory
press conference after being named
MLB's first Black manager in fall of 1974

1. Who was the first major leaguer to win the Most Valuable Player Award in both leagues?

2. What country won the inaugural World Baseball Classic in 2006?

3. Who was the first player to hit for the cycle in both leagues?

4. Can you name the first catcher to catch two perfect games?

5. Who was the first player in big league history to post a season with 45 or more homers while batting below .250?

6. When the American League first expanded in 1961, which two clubs joined the Junior Circuit?

7. Who was the first big leaguer to lead both leagues in stolen bases in separate seasons?

8. On May 28, 1995, what two teams combined to hit 12 home runs, the first time in history a pair of clubs have hit a dozen round-trippers in one contest?

9. Who was the first player to join the 3,000 Hit Club in the twentieth century?

10. On June 29, 1990, two pitchers for the first time tossed no-hitters on the same date. Can you name the pair of no-hit hurlers?

11. In 1980, for the first time in the twentieth century, five players stole 75 or more bases. Can you name this base-stealing quartet?

12. When was the first year that MLB included a wild card game in their postseason playoff format?

13. Who became the first big league player to grace the cover of *TIME* magazine?

14. Who was the first—and only—left-handed throwing, right-handed batting big leaguer with over 200 career home runs?

15. Can you name the first left-handed US President to throw out an opening day ceremonial first pitch?

16. Who was the first three-generation family in big league history?

17. Who was the first person to get hits for two different teams in two different cities on the same day?

18. Who was the first National Leaguer to post a season with a .300 batting average and at least 30 home runs and 100 runs batted in?

19. What two clubs played in the first night game in major league history on May 24, 1935?

20. Who, on May 6, 1953, tossed a no-hitter in his first big league start?

21. What year did the "save" become an official MLB statistic?

22. Can you name the longtime shortstop who, in 1965, became the first player in big league history to have played nine positions in one game?

23. Where was the first big league regular season game played outside of North America?

24. Who was the first native of the Dominican Republic to appear in a big league game?

25. Who was named the first All-Star Game MVP in 1962?

26. What team was the first to draw at least four million fans in one season?

27. Who became the first pitcher in the modern era to walk nine batters in a complete-game, nine-inning no-hitter?

28. What team was the first to include numbers on the back of major league jerseys?

29. Who was the first Latin American-born player to win an MVP Award?

30. Who was the first player selected in the first amateur draft in 1965?

31. In what year was the first World Series night game played?

32. Which Texas Rangers left-hander was taken with the first pick of the 1973 amateur draft and famously made his major league debut that same season?

33. Can you name the Hall of Fame pitcher who hit a home run in his first major league at-bat, in 1952, but never hit another in his twenty-one-year big league career?

34. Who was the first African American to manage in the major leagues?

35. Who was the first big league player to reach 2,000 career RBI?

36. Who was the first player to have his number retired by a team?

37. Who was the first Canadian-born player elected to the Hall of Fame?

38. Who hit the first home run in All-Star Game history in 1933?

39. Who, in 1990, became the first father-son combination to appear as starting teammates in a big league game?

40. In what year were the first Gold Glove Awards bestowed?

41. Who was the first pitcher to win the Cy Young Award and Most Valuable Player Award in the same season?

42. Who was the first relief pitcher to win the American League Cy Young Award?

43. Who was the first batter to hit a home run for his 3,000th major league hit?

44. Who, in 1947, became the first African American player in the history of the American League?

45. Who was the first player to hit a pinch-hit homer in the World Series?

46. Which player hit the first home run at Yankee Stadium when it opened on April 18, 1923?

47. What team won the first championship of the All-American Girls Professional Baseball League in 1943?

48. Who managed the Mets to their first World Series title in 1969?

49. Who is the first player in the modern era of big league baseball to play for at least fourteen different teams?

50. Who, in 1966, became the first African American umpire in American League history?

Larry Doby became the first African American to play in the American League when he debuted with the Cleveland Indians in 1947.

Photo credit: National Baseball Hall of Fame and Museum

Answers

1. Frank Robinson won the NL MVP Award playing
    for the Reds in 1961, and later won the AL MVP
    with the Orioles in 1966.

2. Japan defeated Cuba 10-6, winning the first
    World Baseball Classic.

3. Bob Watson, who achieved the feat in the
    National League with the Houston Astros in
    1977 and in the American League with the
    Boston Red Sox in 1979.

4. Ron Hassey caught Len Barker's perfecto on
    May 15, 1981, and Dennis Martínez's masterpiece
    on July 28, 1991.

5. In 1962, Harmon Killebrew slugged 48 home runs while compiling a .243 average.

6. The Los Angeles Angels and the Washington Senators (now the Texas Rangers) joined the AL in 1961.

7. The Tigers Ron LeFlore led the American League in stolen bases with 68 in 1978 and led the National League with 97 stolen bases for Montreal in 1980.

8. The White Sox outslugged the Tigers 14-12 on May 28, 1995, combining to hit 12 homers.

9. Honus Wagner reached the milestone on June 9, 1914, with the Pirates.

10. Oakland pitcher Dave Stewart threw a 5-0 no-hitter against Toronto. Later that evening, Dodgers' southpaw Fernando Valenzuela repeated the feat, shutting out the Cardinals without a hit, 6-0.

11. Dave Collins (79), Rickey Henderson (100), Ron LeFlore (97), Omar Moreno (96), and Willie Wilson (79) each stole over 75 bases in 1980.

12. Two wild card teams in each league were added to the MLB playoff format for the 2012 postseason, with the Orioles going up against the Rangers and the Cardinals playing the Braves in their respective leagues.

13. George Sisler of the St. Louis Browns appeared on the March 30, 1925, cover of *Time* magazine.

14. Rickey Henderson is the only right-handed batting, left-handed throwing player to hit 200 career homers.

15. Harry S. Truman became the first "lefty" US President to throw out an opening day first pitch in 1946.

16. The Boones: grandfather Ray (1948-1960), father Bob (1972-1990), and sons Bret (1992-2005) and Aaron (1997-2003, 2005-2009).

17. On August 4, 1982, Joel Youngblood of the New York Mets singled at the Chicago Cubs in the afternoon, was traded to Montreal in the middle of the game, and then singled for the Expos in a night game at the Philadelphia Phillies.

18. St. Louis Cardinals second baseman Rogers Hornsby accomplished the feat in 1922.

19. The Philadelphia Phillies lost to the Cincinnati Reds 2-1 under the lights at Crosley Field in the first night game in major league history.

20. On May 6, 1953, St. Louis Browns rookie pitcher Bobo Holloman tossed a no-hitter in his first big league start against the Athletics and never completed another game.

21. The "save" became an official MLB statistic in 1969. The Minnesota Twins Ron Perranoski led baseball with 31 saves that season.

Lou Gehrig became the first player to have his uniform number retired when the Yankees retired his #4 jersey in 1939.

Photo credit: Charles Conlon/National Baseball Hall of Fame and Museum

22. Bert Campaneris of the Kansas City Athletics played nine positions in a single game on September 8, 1965, against the California Angels.

23. On March 29, 2000, the Cubs and Mets opened the season at the Tokyo Dome in Tokyo, Japan, for the first regular season game ever played outside of North America.

24. Third baseman Ozzie Virgil Sr., who made his debut with the NY Giants in 1956.

25. The LA Dodgers Maury Wills, who scored two of the National League's three runs in a 3-1 victory.

26. 1991 Toronto Blue Jays drew 4,001,527 fans to the SkyDome.

27. While pitching for the Marlins on May 12, 2001, starting pitcher A.J. Burnett tossed a no-hitter against the Padres. He became the first pitcher in the modern era to walk nine batters in a complete-game, nine-inning no-hitter.

28. The Indians debuted their numbered jerseys on April 16, 1929, one day before the Yankees.

29. Zoilo Versalles, born in Cuba, won the AL MVP Award with the Twins in 1965 after leading the league with 126 runs scored, 45 doubles, and 12 triples.

30. Rick Monday was selected number one overall by the Kansas City Athletics in the 1965 amateur draft.

31. The first World Series night game was played in 1971 at Three Rivers Stadium when the Pittsburgh Pirates hosted the Baltimore Orioles.

32. Texas native David Clyde made his major league debut with the Rangers in 1973, defeating the Minnesota Twins 4-3.

33. Hoyt Wilhelm, who homered in his first at-bat with the Giants on April 18, 1952.

34. Frank Robinson became the first African American manager in the majors when he was hired as player/manager for the Cleveland Indians in 1975.

35. Chicago Cubs first baseman Cap Anson became the first major leaguer to reach the milestone, finishing his career with 2,075 RBI.

36. Lou Gehrig was the first player to have his uniform number retired when the Yankees retired his number (4) in 1939.

37. Ferguson Jenkins, born in Chatham, Ontario, became the first Canadian-born player elected to the Hall of Fame in 1991.

38. Babe Ruth, who homered off the Cardinals Bill Hallahan in the first All-Star Game in 1933.

39. On August 31, 1990, Ken Griffey Sr. and Ken Griffey Jr. became the first father-son combination to appear as teammates in a major league game. The Griffeys and the Seattle Mariners defeated the Kansas City Royals, 5-2.

40. The Gold Glove Awards were first given in 1957.

41. The Dodgers Don Newcombe won both awards in 1956.

42. Yankees closer Sparky Lyle won the 1977 AL Cy Young Award after finishing the season with a 13-5 record, a 2.17 ERA, and 26 saves.

43. On August 7, 1999, Wade Boggs became the first player to homer for his 3,000th hit.

44. Larry Doby made his debut with the Cleveland Indians in 1947, becoming the first African American to play in the AL.

45. On Oct. 2, 1947, the Yankees' Yogi Berra became the first player to hit a pinch-hit home run in the World Series when he homered against the Dodgers.

46. In the first game at Yankee Stadium, Babe Ruth homered off the Red Sox Howard Ehmke in the bottom of the third inning.

47. The Racine Belles won the championship in the AAGPBL's inaugural season, sweeping the Kenosha Comets in three games.

48. Gil Hodges managed the "Miracle Mets" to their first championship, defeating the Orioles in the 1969 World Series.

49. Edwin Jackson, who played for the Dodgers, Rays, Tigers, Diamondbacks, White Sox, Cardinals, Nationals, Cubs, Braves, Marlins, Padres, Orioles, Athletics, and Blue Jays.

50. In 1966, after years as an umpire in the minor leagues, Emmett Ashford became the first African American umpire in AL history.

In 1914, the Pirates' Honus Wagner became the first player in the twentieth century to record 3,000 hits.

Photo credit: National Baseball Hall of Fame and Museum

Chapter 2

First-Year Phenoms

"Kid, when you kick a water bucket, never kick it with your toes. Always use the side of your foot."

—Lefty Grove, on watching a rookie pitcher
hurting his foot kicking a water bucket

1. Who was the youngest player in MLB history?

2. Who was the first pitcher to win the Rookie of the Year Award and the Cy Young Award in the same season?

3. Who was the first player from a first-year expansion team to win the Rookie of the Year Award?

4. What franchise holds the record for most players to win the Rookie of the Year?

5. What two future Hall of Famers were named Rookie of the Year in 1967?

6. In only his fifth career start, which rookie pitcher tied an MLB record, striking out 20 batters in a game against the Astros?

7. Only one Rookie of the Year Award was presented in both 1947 and 1948. Jackie Robinson won the 1947 award. Who was named Rookie of the Year in 1948?

8. What player was named the NL Rookie of the Year after leading the Giants to their first World Series title in San Francisco?

9. What was the first year that two future Hall of Famers were named Rookie of the Year?

10. Who was the first Cuban-born player to win the Rookie of the Year Award?

11. Who is the only modern era rookie to steal at least 100 bases?

12. Who was the first American League player to win the Rookie of the Year Award?

13. Which batter holds the record for most RBI by a National League rookie?

14. Who holds the record for most home runs by a rookie?

15. Who is the youngest player to ever start an All-Star Game?

16. What player won the 2007 AL Rookie of the Year and followed that with the 2008 AL MVP Award?

17. Who was the first left-handed relief pitcher to win Rookie of the Year honors?

18. Who was the first American League player to be unanimously named Rookie of the Year?

19. What two players finished tied for the 1976 NL Rookie of the Year Award?

20. Who was the first Latin American-born player to win a Rookie of the Year Award?

21. What pitcher holds the record for most appearances as a rookie?

22. Which Indians pitcher set an American League rookie record with 245 strikeouts in 1955?

23. What two future Hall of Famers won the Rookie of the Year Awards in 1977?

24. Who was the first Japanese native to play in the major leagues?

25. What two players share the AL rookie record for doubles with 47?

26. Who was the first rookie to appear in at least 162 games in one season?

27. What player was named the 1959 NL Rookie of the Year despite playing in only 52 games that season?

28. Who is the only rookie ever to record 700 at-bats in one season?

29. What two players tied for American League Rookie of the Year honors in 1979?

30. Who holds the rookie record for most saves in one season?

31. Who was the first player to win the Rookie of the Year and Most Valuable Player Awards in the same season?

32. Which team is the only franchise to have five Rookies of the Year in a row?

33. Who was the first native of the Dominican Republic to be named Rookie of the Year?

34. Who became the first Pittsburgh Pirates player to win the Rookie of the Year Award— more than fifty years after the award was established?

35. What three Oakland A's players won the AL Rookie of the Year Award from 1986–88?

36. Which rookie stole 71 bases in just 88 games during the 1981 season?

37. Who was the first Japanese player to be named Rookie of the Year?

38. Who was the 1987 NL Rookie of the Year who posted a rookie record 34-game hitting streak?

39. Who holds the rookie record for most runs scored in one season?

40. Who is the only Rookie of the Year Award winner to post 20 wins during his rookie season?

41. What player set a rookie record with 49 home runs in 1987, besting the previous mark by 11?

42. What two players share the record for most total bases by a rookie?

43. Among catchers, who holds the rookie record for RBI?

44. Among Live Ball (post-1919) era players who qualified for the batting title, which American League rookie posted the highest batting average?

45. What was the first year that both the NL and AL Rookie of the Year Award winners were pitchers?

46. Who is the only rookie to post a season with at least 30 home runs and 40 stolen bases?

47. Who holds the rookie record for most walks
in a season?

48. Who was the first pitcher to win a Rookie of the
Year Award?

49. Who holds the rookie record for most RBI in
one season?

50. Which future Hall of Famer led the National
League with 367 innings pitched as a
rookie in 1911?

Mike Trout became the only rookie to hit 30 home runs and steal 40 bases on his way to winning the Rookie of the Year Award in 2012.

Photo credit: Jean Fruth/National Baseball Hall of Fame and Museum

Answers

1. Joe Nuxhall became the youngest player in major league history when he made his debut for the Reds at the age of fifteen in 1944. It was the only game he appeared in that season, and he wouldn't pitch in the majors again until 1952.

2. Fernando Valenzuela won the NL Rookie of the Year and Cy Young Awards with the Dodgers in 1981.

3. Lou Piniella, who won the AL Rookie of the Year Award with the Royals in 1969.

4. The Dodgers with eighteen winners of the award.

5. The Twins Rod Carew and the Mets Tom Seaver won the Rookie of the Year Award for their respective leagues in 1967.

6. The Cubs Kerry Wood tied the major league mark by striking out 20 batters in a complete-game shutout of the Astros on May 6, 1998.

7. Shortstop Alvin Dark of the Boston Braves was the second recipient of the award in 1948.

8. Buster Posey, who won the award in 2010 after hitting .305 with 18 homers and 67 RBI.

9. 1956, with Luis Aparicio winning the award in the AL and Frank Robinson in the NL.

10. Tony Oliva, who was born in Pinar del Rio, Cuba, won the award with the Twins in 1964.

11. St. Louis outfielder Vince Coleman, who stole 110 bases for the Cardinals in 1985.

12. The St. Louis Browns Roy Sievers won the first AL Rookie of the Year Award in 1949.

13. Albert Pujols, who drove in 130 runs for the Cardinals in 2001.

14. Mets first baseman Pete Alonso set the rookie record for home runs with 53 in 2019.

15. Twenty-year-old Al Kaline became the youngest player to start an All-Star Game in 1955.

16. Red Sox second baseman Dustin Pedroia.

17. Dodgers' lefty relief pitcher Steve Howe won the award in 1980.

18. Red Sox catcher Carlton Fisk was the unanimous selection as the AL Rookie of the Year in 1972.

19. Pat Zachry of the Reds and Butch Metzger of the Padres.

20. Shortstop Luis Aparicio, born in Maracaibo, Venezuela, won the award in 1956 with the Chicago White Sox.

21. Wayne Granger made the most appearances as a rookie, pitching in 90 games in 1969. Granger was also the first pitcher ever to appear in at least 90 games in one season.

22. Indians' hurler Herb Score led the AL in strikeouts in 1955, also setting the mark for rookie pitchers.

23. The Orioles Eddie Murray won the award in the AL, with the Cubs Andre Dawson winning the NL award.

Twenty-year-old Al Kaline became the youngest player to start an All-Star Game when he was selected to start the 1955 game.

Photo credit: Don Wingfield/National Baseball Hall of Fame and Museum

24. Masanori Murakami debuted with the San Francisco Giants on September 1, 1964.

25. Red Sox center fielder Fred Lynn belted 47 doubles in 1975, and Yankee third baseman Miguel Andújar tied the mark in 2018.

26. Jake Wood appeared in all 162 games for the Tigers in 1961.

27. In 1959, Willie McCovey of the Giants hit .354 with 13 homers and 38 RBI in 52 games.

28. Juan Samuel of the Phillies recorded 701 at-bats in 1984, the first rookie to do so.

29. John Castino of the Twins and Alfredo Griffin of the Blue Jays.

30. Craig Kimbrel, who saved 46 games for the Braves in 2011.

31. Fred Lynn of the Red Sox won the American League Rookie of the Year Award and Most Valuable Player Award in 1975.

32. The Los Angeles Dodgers had five straight Rookies of the Year from 1992–96: Eric Karros, Mike Piazza, Raul Mondesi, Hideo Nomo, and Todd Hollandsworth.

33. Toronto shortstop Alfredo Griffin became the first Dominican-born player to win the award in 1979.

34. The Pirates had their first Rookie of the Year winner in 2004 when outfielder Jason Bay won the award.

35. José Canseco, Mark McGwire, and Walt Weiss won the award in three consecutive years.

36. Tim Raines of the Expos swiped 71 bases during the strike abbreviated 1981 season.

37. Hideo Nomo of the Dodgers won the award in 1995.

38. Padres' catcher Benito Santiago won the award in 1987.

39. Lloyd Waner, who scored 133 runs for the Pirates in 1927.

40. Bob Grim of the Yankees, who posted a 20-6 record in 1954.

41. The Athletics Mark McGwire homered 49 times in 1987, besting the previous record of 38 home runs held by Wally Berger and Frank Robinson.

42. The Indians Hal Trosky (1934) and Twins Tony Oliva (1964) both had 374 total bases in their rookie seasons.

43. Dodger backstop Mike Piazza set the record with 112 RBI in 1993.

44. Ichiro Suzuki, who joined the Seattle Mariners from the Orix Blue Wave of the Japanese Pacific League, set the mark with a .350 batting average in 2001.

45. Pitchers Joe Black of the Dodgers and Harry Byrd of the Athletics both won the award in their respective leagues in 1952.

46. Center fielder Mike Trout accomplished the feat in 2012 with the Angels.

47. Yankee slugger Aaron Judge set the mark drawing 127 walks in 2017.

48. The Dodgers Don Newcombe became the first pitcher to win the Rookie of the Year Award in 1949 when he posted a 17-8 record and a 3.17 ERA.

49. Outfielder Ted Williams set the rookie mark after driving in 145 runs for the Red Sox in 1939.

50. In 1911, Grover Cleveland Alexander had one of the greatest rookie seasons ever by a pitcher, tossing 367 innings with a 28-13 record, 2.57 ERA, 31 complete games, and 7 shutouts.

The Dodgers had five straight Rookie of the Year Award winners from 1992–1996, including catcher Mike Piazza who won the award in 1993.

Photo credit: National Baseball Hall of Fame and Museum

Chapter 3

Legendary Sluggers

"Cadillacs are down at the end of the bat."

—Ralph Kiner

1. Who holds the major league record for most career triples hit with 309?

2. Who was the last American League batter to have at least 400 total bases in one season?

3. Who holds the record for most home runs as a shortstop?

4. Which two players reached the 50-home-run mark in 1938, the first season to feature two players with at least 50 long balls?

5. What batter leads all Canadian-born players with 383 big league round-trippers?

6. Who is the only major leaguer to post a season with 40 or more homers, 40 or more doubles, and 40 or more stolen bases?

7. Who holds the record for most career RBI?

8. Who holds the all-time record for most home runs as a first baseman?

9. George Brett hit a home run off of which pitcher during the infamous "Pine Tar" game?

10. Which college did Hall of Famer Frank Thomas attend?

11. In 1947, which slugger became the first player to hit at least 50 home runs while striking out fewer than 50 times?

12. What batter led all major leaguers in home runs (326) and runs batted in (1,031) during the 1950s (1950–1959)?

13. Can you name the Hall of Famer who drove in 12 runs in a single big league game?

14. Who held the record for most home runs in a season before Babe Ruth broke it during the 1919 season in which he slugged 29 homers?

15. Who was the first major leaguer to clout 100 or more home runs for three different clubs?

16. Who holds the big league record for most career home runs hit as a second baseman?

17. Babe Ruth won one American League batting title in his career, in 1924, but lost out on his only chance at a batting Triple Crown that season when this future Hall of Famer had five more RBI. Who was he?

18. Who hit "The Shot Heard 'Round the World"?

19. Who was the first big leaguer to hit at least 30 home runs in his final season?

20. Who is the only American League catcher to lead his league in triples in one season?

21. On August 11, 1929, Babe Ruth became the first player to hit 500 career home runs. Who was the second to reach the milestone?

22. In the twenty-four seasons from 1966 through 1989, only one big league player reached the 50-home-run mark. Who was he?

23. Which Indians third baseman was edged out for the 1953 American League Batting Triple Crown by one one-thousandth of a batting point?

24. Which player has hit the most grand slams in MLB history?

25. Which Red Sox outfielder won the American League Batting Triple Crown in 1967?

26. Who is the only player to win four straight league MVP awards?

27. Which batter topped the 1969 Amazing Mets with 26 home runs and 76 RBI?

28. Who hit the last home run at Ebbets Field?

29. Who is the only player to hit at least 60 home runs in three or more seasons?

30. Which Indians player became the first player in big league history with at least 50 doubles and 50 homers in one season?

31. Which American League slugger hit 51 home runs in 1990, a season after playing for the Hanshin Tigers in Japan?

32. Can you name the slugger who was the first to hit 40-or-more homers in a season in both leagues?

33. Which slugging shortstop won back-to-back National League MVP Awards in 1958 and 1959?

34. Three batters share the MLB record with home runs in eight straight games. Don Mattingly and Ken Griffey Jr. are two of the three batters. Who set the standard that still stands with home runs in eight straight games in 1956?

35. Who is the only National League player to win two batting Triple Crowns?

36. Which Hall of Famer holds the record for most home runs by a catcher?

37. Whose ninth-inning home run in Game 5 of the 1976 American League Championship Series propelled the Yankees to their first World Series berth in twelve seasons?

38. Which pitcher gave up Reggie Jackson's titanic, rooftop home run at the 1971 All-Star Game?

39. In 1933, two players won the batting Triple Crown—the only year that has featured a batting Triple Crown winner in both leagues. Who were these two future Hall of Famers?

40. Who was the first player to post a 30-home-run season in both the National and American leagues?

41. Who, on April 17, 1976, blasted four consecutive home runs in a game at Wrigley Field?

42. Which Hall of Famer homered in their final at-bat on September 28, 1960?

43. Who, in 1922, became the first big league player to hit at least 30 home runs and steal at least 30 bases?

44. Who, on October 1, 1950, hit a game-winning home run in the 10th inning to clinch the National League pennant for the "Whiz Kids"?

45. What pair of brothers holds the record for most career home runs combined?

46. With what team did Jim Thome hit his 600th career home run?

47. After the 1935 season, the last of Babe Ruth's career, who was in second place on the all-time home run list behind the Babe and his 714 home runs?

48. Who is the only catcher to lead the majors in home runs in the modern era?

49. Who won the first All-Star Game Home Run Derby?

50. Who hit the most career home runs in extra innings?

Hank Aaron holds the career record for RBI with 2,297.

Photo credit: National Baseball Hall of Fame and Museum

Answers

1. Sam Crawford smacked 309 triples during his career with the Reds and Tigers.

2. Jim Rice collected 406 total bases with the Red Sox in 1978.

3. Cal Ripken Jr. slugged 345 home runs playing shortstop for the Orioles.

4. The Tigers Hank Greenberg (58) and Red Sox Jimmie Foxx (50) both reached the 50-homer milestone in 1938.

5. Larry Walker who was born in Maple Ridge, British Columbia.

6. In 2006, Washington's Alfonso Soriano hit 46 homers, 41 doubles and stole 41 bases.

7. Hank Aaron, who finished his twenty-three-year career with 2,297 RBI.

8. Mark McGwire, who slugged 566 home runs as a first baseman with the Athletics and Cardinals.

9. Brett hit a dramatic 2-run homer off reliever Goose Gossage in the top of the ninth inning, giving the Royals a 5-4 lead.

10. Frank Thomas attended Auburn University, playing both baseball and football for the Tigers.

11. Johnny Mize hit 51 homers while whiffing only 42 times for the Giants in 1947.

12. Dodgers' outfielder Duke Snider led all major leaguers in home runs (326) and runs batted in (1,031) during the 1950s.

13. On September 16, 1924, in a game against the Dodgers, Jim Bottomley of the Cardinals drove in a record 12 runs with two homers, a double, and three singles.

14. Ned Williams held the record for most home runs in a season, setting the mark in 1884 when he hit 27 round-trippers for the Chicago White Stockings.

15. Reggie Jackson slugged over 100 home runs for the Athletics, Yankees, and Angels.

16. Jeff Kent hit 349 home runs as a second baseman, more than any other player at the position.

17. Goose Goslin of the Washington Senators led the AL with 129 RBI in 1924, five more than Babe Ruth's total of 124.

18. In 1951, Bobby Thomson hit the "Shot Heard 'Round the World" to win the final game of the three-game playoff series between the Giants and the Dodgers, giving the Giants the NL Pennant.

19. Dave Kingman hit 35 home runs in his final season with the Athletics in 1986.

20. Carlton Fisk led the American League in triples in 1972 with nine, tying Oakland's Joe Rudi for the top spot.

21. The Red Sox Jimmie Foxx became the second player to hit 500 career home runs on September 24, 1940, when he homered off George Caster of the Athletics.

22. George Foster, who slugged 52 homers for the Reds in 1977.

23. Al Rosen led the AL with 43 home runs and 145 RBI in 1953, but his .336 batting average was just shy of the mark of .337 posted by the Senators Mickey Vernon.

24. Alex Rodríguez, who hit 25 grand slams during his twenty-two-year career.

25. Red Sox left fielder Carl Yastrzemski won the AL Batting Triple Crown in 1967 with 44 home runs, 121 RBI, and a .326 batting average.

26. The Giants Barry Bonds won four straight NL MVP Awards from 2001–2004.

27. Outfielder Tommie Agee led the World Series Champion Mets in home runs and RBI in 1969.

28. The Brooklyn Dodgers Duke Snider hit the last home run at Ebbets Field when he homered against the Phillies on September 22, 1957.

Bobby Thomson kisses the bat he used to hit the "Shot Heard 'Round the World," a walk-off home run that clinched the 1951 pennant for the NY Giants.

Photo credit: National Baseball Hall of Fame and Museum

29. Sammy Sosa hit 66 homers in 1998, 63 homers in 1999, and 64 homers in 2001.

30. Albert Belle hit 52 doubles and 50 home runs in 1995.

31. Cecil Fielder of the Tigers swatted 51 homers with 132 RBI while scoring 104 runs in 1990.

32. Darrell Evans hit 41 homers with the NL's Atlanta Braves in 1973 and hit 40 homers with the AL's Detroit Tigers in 1985.

33. The Cubs' Ernie Banks won the NL MVP in 1958 and again in 1959.

34. In 1956 first baseman Dale Long of the Pirates was the first player to homer in eight straight games.

35. Rogers Hornsby of the Cardinals won the NL Batting Triple Crown in both 1922 and 1925.

36. Mike Piazza hit 396 of his 427 career home runs as a catcher, the most of any backstop in history.

37. Chris Chambliss homered off the Royals Mark Littell giving the Yankees a 7-6 victory in the final game of the 1976 ALCS.

38. Dock Ellis of the Pittsburgh Pirates gave up the towering blast to Reggie Jackson in the third inning of the 1971 All-Star Game.

39. The Philadelphia Athletics Jimmie Foxx, and the Philadelphia Phillies Chuck Klein won the batting Triple Crown in their respective leagues in 1933.

40. Dick Stuart swatted 35 homers for the Pittsburgh Pirates in 1961 and 42 homers for the Boston Red Sox in 1963.

41. Mike Schmidt of the Philadelphia Phillies blasted four consecutive home runs in a wild 18-16 win over the Chicago Cubs.

42. Ted Williams homered in his final at-bat, ending his career with 521 career home runs.

43. Ken Williams of the St. Louis Browns slugged 39 home runs and swiped 37 bases during the 1922 season.

44. Left fielder Dick Sisler homered against the Dodgers Don Newcombe to clinch the 1950 NL pennant for the Phillies.

45. Hank Aaron (755) and his brother Tommie Aaron (13) combined for 768 homers.

46. Thome clubbed his 599th and 600th home runs in the same game against the Detroit Tigers as a member of the Minnesota Twins.

47. When Babe Ruth retired from baseball, Lou Gehrig was in second place on the career home run list with 378 round-trippers.

48. Johnny Bench of the Cincinnati Reds did it twice, leading the majors in home runs in 1970 and 1972.

49. Dave Parker of the Cincinnati Reds won the first Home Run Derby held during the 1985 All-Star Game at the Metrodome.

50. Willie Mays hit 22 of his 660 career home runs in extra innings.

During his career, Wille Mays slugged 22 home runs in extra innings, more than any other player.

Photo credit: National Baseball Hall of Fame and Museum

Chapter 4

Historic Hurlers

"Anybody's best pitch is the one the batters ain't hitting that day."

—Christy Mathewson, *The Sporting News*, August 6, 1948

1. Who is the only pitcher with at least 200 career wins and 150 career saves?

2. What is Hall of Famer pitcher Cy Young's given first name?

3. Who holds the record for most career home runs hit by a pitcher?

4. Who is the only pitcher to have won three Major League Baseball All-Star Games?

5. How many big league no-hitters did fire-balling righty Nolan Ryan toss?

6. Which pitcher led the American League in shutouts (9) and earned-run average (1.60) in 1968?

7. Who is the only Mexican-born major league pitcher with at least 150 career victories?

8. In 1974, which pitcher became the first to notch 3,000 career strikeouts since Walter Johnson in 1923?

9. Which pitcher has won the most Gold Glove Awards, with eighteen total?

10. Which Yankees pitcher hurled two no-hitters during the 1951 season?

11. Which pitcher has more postseason wins than any other?

12. Which pitcher won or saved the All-Star Game each season from 1978 through 1981?

13. Who was the losing pitcher for the Dodgers in Don Larsen's perfect game in the 1956 World Series?

14. Which two Hall of Fame pitchers finished their careers with exactly 300 wins?

15. Who was the last pitcher legally allowed to throw the spitball?

16. Which pitcher has the most career victories in New York Yankees history?

17. Who are the only two brothers to win the Cy Young Award?

18. The 1971 Baltimore Orioles featured a rotation with four 20-game winners. Which one of those pitchers led the Orioles with 21 wins?

19. Who is the pitcher who holds the American League mark for wins and complete games in a season, both accomplished in the same season?

20. Which pitcher led the American League in strikeouts 12 times?

---

21. Can you name the Detroit pitcher who finished with a 5-19 record in 1952, with two of his wins the result of no-hitters?

22. Can you name the Hall of Fame pitcher who led the National League in both wins and losses in 1979?

23. Who was the last pitcher to win 30 or more games in a season?

24. Who is the only pitcher to strike out at least 30 batters in one World Series?

25. Which Hall of Fame pitcher threw a perfect game on Father's Day in 1964?

26. For what college team did Tom Seaver star on before his major league career?

27. With which basketball team did future Hall of Famer Bob Gibson play before his big league pitching career?

28. Hall of Famer Sandy Koufax won the Cy Young Award in 1963, 1965, and 1966. Who won the award in 1964?

29. Which Hall of Fame pitcher is the all-time leader in shutouts with 110?

30. Which White Sox pitcher worked 376.2 innings in 1972, the most of any pitcher since 1920?

31. How many scheduled starting assignments did Hall of Fame pitcher Don Sutton miss in his entire career?

32. Which pitcher led the 1962 New York Mets with 10 victories, a quarter of the team's total wins?

33. Which Orioles pitcher struck out 11 batters in a relief appearance in Game 1 of the 1966 World Series?

34. Which Hall of Fame pitcher managed the Colorado Silver Bullets women's barnstorming team in the 1990s?

35. Which New York Yankees pitcher tossed a no-hitter on July 4, 1983, at Yankee Stadium?

36. Which pitcher holds the modern rookie record for most strikeouts in a season with 276?

37. Which Hall of Fame pitcher holds the record for most career ERA titles with nine?

38. Which NY Mets pitcher tossed the first no-hitter in franchise history?

39. Which Hall of Fame pitcher holds the record for most consecutive victories?

40. Can you name the pitcher who won sixteen consecutive Gold Glove Awards for fielding excellence?

41. Who was the last pitcher to work at least 300 innings in one season?

42. Who, with his twenty-six appearances for the A's in 2015, became the first full-time switch-pitcher in modern big league history?

43. Who was the pitcher who not only tossed a no-hitter but also hit two homers in a memorable 1971 game?

44. Can you name the Hall of Famer who was the first pitcher to have at least 100 strikeouts in 20 straight seasons?

45. Roger Clemens won Cy Young Awards with which teams?

46. Which Hall of Famer set the American League record for wins by a left-handed pitcher in one season with 31 in 1931?

47. Can you name the hurler who led the National League in strikeouts for seven straight seasons, from 1922 to 1928?

48. Which Hall of Fame pitcher holds the record for most wins by a left-hander?

49. While Hall of Fame pitcher Nolan Ryan holds the big league record with seven no-hitters, who is second on the all-time list?

50. Who hurled the first opening day no-hitter in major league history?

Fireballer Nolan Ryan pitched seven no-hitters in his twenty-seven-year career—more than any other pitcher to date.

Photo credit: National Baseball Hall of Fame and Museum

Answers

1. John Smoltz, who pitched most of his career as a starter, but later spent four seasons as a closer after developing arm problems.

2. Cy Young, the winningest pitcher in major league history, was born Denton True Young.

3. Wes Ferrell hit more home runs than any other pitcher, homering 38 times in his career.

4. Lefty Gomez of the Yankees took home All-Star Game victories in 1933, 1935, and 1937.

5. Nolan Ryan threw a total of seven career no-hitters; four while playing for the Angels, one with the Astros, and two with the Rangers.

6. Luis Tiant led the AL in shutouts and earned-run average in 1968, while posting a 21-9 record for the Indians.

7. Fernando Valenzuela, who won 173 games over his seventeen-year career.

8. The Cardinals Bob Gibson reached the milestone on July 17, 1974, against the Reds, and totaled 3,117 strikeouts in his career.

9. Pitcher Greg Maddux was awarded the Gold Glove eighteen times during his twenty-three-year career with the Cubs, Braves, Dodgers, and Padres.

10. On July 12, 1951, Allie Reynolds tossed a no-hitter against the Indians, then a few months later, on September 28, he threw his second no-hitter of the season against the Red Sox.

11. Andy Pettitte won 19 games in 32 postseason series with the Yankees and Astros.

12. Bruce Sutter won the 1978 and 1979 games, while recording the save in the 1980 and 1981 games.

13. The Dodgers Sal Maglie was the hard-luck loser in the 2-0 Yankees victory.

14. Lefty Grove and Early Wynn both finished their Hall of Fame careers with exactly 300 wins.

15. Burleigh Grimes was the last pitcher allowed to throw a spitball after the pitch was outlawed in 1920.

16. Whitey Ford, who won 236 games in his 16 year big league career, all with the Yankees.

17. Gaylord Perry and Jim Perry are the only brothers to both win the Cy Young Award. Gaylord won it with the Indians (1972) and the Padres (1978), and his brother Jim won the award with the Twins (1970).

18. Dave McNally won 21 games in 1971, with Mike Cuellar, Pat Dobson, and Jim Palmer each winning 20 games that season.

19. In 1904, Jack Chesbro of the American League's New York Highlanders had 41 wins and 48 complete games.

20. Pitching for the Washington Senators, the right-handed Walter Johnson led the AL in strikeouts in 1910, 1912–1919, 1921, and 1923–1924.

21. In 1952, Detroit's Virgil Trucks tossed no-hitters against the Washington Senators on May 15 and against the New York Yankees on August 25.

22. Pitching for the Atlanta Braves in 1979, forty-year-old knuckleballer Phil Niekro went 21-20 with a 3.39 ERA.

23. The Tigers Denny McLain went 31-6 with a 1.96 ERA in 1968.

24. Bob Gibson twice struck out 30 batters in one World Series, setting a record with 31 strikeouts in the 1964 Fall Classic and then breaking his own record with 35 strikeouts in 1968.

25. The Phillies Jim Bunning pitched a perfect game against the Mets on June 21, 1964.

Denton True Young, better known as Cy Young, holds the record for career victories with 511.

Photo credit: Charles Conlon/National Baseball Hall of Fame and Museum

26. Tom Seaver pitched one season for the USC
Trojans, posting a 10-2 mark with a 2.47 ERA in 1965.

27. Bob Gibson was recruited to play with the
Harlem Globetrotters during his collegiate
career at Creighton, playing for the team in
1957 before joining the Cardinals.

28. Dean Chance of the Angels went 20-9 in 1964.
Only one Cy Young Award per season was given
out from 1956-66. Starting in 1967, Cy Young
Awards were presented in each league.

29. Walter Johnson recorded 110 shutouts in his
career with the Washington Senators, the only
pitcher with more than 100 career shutouts.

30. Knuckleballer Wilbur Wood started 49 games
in 1972 for the White Sox, going 24-17 while
working 376.2 innings.

31. Don Sutton never missed a scheduled turn in the rotation in twenty-three seasons.

32. Roger Craig went 10-24 during the Mets inaugural season in 1962.

33. Moe Drabowsky relieved starter Dave McNally in the third inning of Game 1 of the 1966 World Series, finishing the game and striking out 11 Dodgers.

34. Phil Niekro managed the Silver Bullets from 1994–1997 before the team folded prior to the start of the 1998 season.

35. Dave Righetti defeated the Red Sox 4-0, recording the Yankees first no-hitter since Don Larsen's perfect game in the 1956 World Series.

36. Dwight Gooden recorded 276 strikeouts during his rookie season with the Mets in 1984.

37. Lefty Grove won a record nine ERA titles pitching for the Athletics and Red Sox.

38. On June 1, 2012, Johan Santana no-hit the St. Louis Cardinals 8-0, recording the first no-hitter in team history.

39. Giants' pitcher Carl Hubbell won 24 straight games during the 1936 and 1937 seasons.

40. Jim Kaat won the Gold Glove Award in 16 straight seasons from 1962–1977 while pitching for the Twins, White Sox, and Phillies.

41. Steve Carlton pitched 304 innings with the Phillies in 1980.

42. Pat Venditte, who made twenty-six appearances with the Athletics in 2015.

43. On June 23, 1971, Rick Wise of the Philadelphia Phillies almost single-handedly defeated the Cincinnati Reds. Wise not only pitched a no-hitter, but also clubbed two home runs in a 4–0 victory.

44. Don Sutton registered at least 100 strikeouts in 20 straight seasons, striking out a total of 3,574 batters in his career.

45. Clemens won Cy Young Awards with the Red Sox (1986, 1987, and 1991), Blue Jays (1997 and 1998), Yankees (2001), and Astros (2004).

46. Lefty Grove recorded an incredible 31-4 record leading the Athletics to the AL pennant in 1931.

47. Dazzy Vance, elected to the Hall of Fame in 1955, led the NL in strikeouts from 1922-1928 while pitching for the Brooklyn Robins.

48. Warren Spahn won 363 games during his twenty-one-year big league career, more than any other southpaw pitcher.

49. Sandy Koufax threw four ho-hitters in his career, the second most in major league history.

50. On April 16, 1940, Hall of Famer Bob Feller of the Cleveland Indians no-hit the White Sox on opening day at Chicago's Comiskey Park.

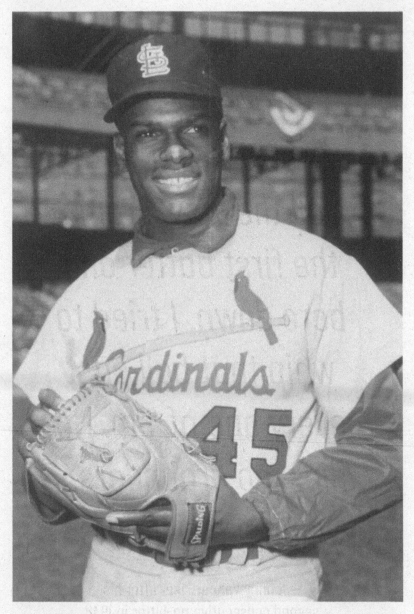

In 1974, Cardinals ace Bob Gibson became the first pitcher to reach 3,000 career strikeouts since Walter Johnson in 1923.

Photo credit: National Baseball Hall of Fame and Museum

Chapter 5

Record Breakers

"I was trying for it all the way. From the first batter on I bore down. I tried to whip that ball past every one of 'em. No flies, no grounders. I wanted strikeouts."

—Johnny Vander Meer after his
second consecutive no-hitter in 1938

1. Who is the shortest player to ever participate in a big league baseball game?

2. Which player holds the record for most appearances at catcher in a career?

3. Which pitcher holds the record for most wins after turning forty years of age?

4. Can you name the Hall of Fame hurler who, on April 22, 1970, set a big league record when he struck out 10 straight batters?

5. Who holds the record for most consecutive games played in the National League?

6. Who are the only pair of brothers to have thrown big league official no-hitters?

7. What speedster is the only player since 1900 to steal 100 bases in three consecutive seasons?

8. Who holds the record for the highest career batting average by a right-handed batter?

9. What member of the Boston Braves is the only pitcher to hit three home runs in one game in modern major league history?

10. Who is the only big leaguer to hit two grand slams in one inning?

11. How many National League batting titles did Hall of Famer Tony Gwynn win?

12. How many consecutive games did Cal Ripken Jr. play for the Orioles from 1982–1998?

13. Who holds the record for most Gold Glove Awards by a first baseman?

14. Who holds the single season record for most triples?

15. Which Hall of Famer is the all-time All-Star Game leader in both home runs and pinch hits?

16. Whose record for hits in a season did Seattle's Ichiro Suzuki break when he collected 262 in 2004?

17. What pitcher earned the most big league wins during the decade of the 1980s?

18. Who holds the record for the most MLB All-Star Game appearances?

19. Which pitcher surrendered Henry Aaron's record-breaking 715th home run in 1974?

20. With what team did outfielder Earl Webb hit his major league record 67 doubles in the 1931 season?

21. Which pitcher tossed back-to-back no-hitters in 1938?

22. What are the only two teams in big league history to feature four 20-game winners?

23. Among position players, who holds the record as the youngest player in big league history during the modern era (post-1900)?

24. Who was the oldest player to appear in a big league game?

25. What two players have represented a record five different teams in the All-Star Game?

26. Which player holds the record for the highest career big league batting average?

27. Which pitcher holds the record for most appearances in one season?

28. Who had the most big league hits in the decade of the 1990s?

29. Who turned the only unassisted triple play in World Series history?

30. Which pitcher set a modern-day record with 383 strikeouts in 1973?

31. Who are the only two pitchers to appear in seven games in one World Series?

32. Which player has appeared in the most MLB games at third base?

33. Who is the only player to record seven hits in a modern nine-inning MLB game?

34. Which pitcher holds the record for the most wins in a season?

35. International League rivals Rochester and Pawtucket played in the longest professional game ever, a 33-inning affair which began on April 18, 1981. What two Hall of Famers played in that game?

36. Who is the only position player to appear in at least a thousand games without being hit by a pitch?

37. Who is the only player to appear in both a World Series game and a Super Bowl game?

38. Who holds the record for most stolen bases in a season by a catcher?

39. Who is the only MLB pitcher to post a season with at least 12 wins and no losses?

40. Who was the youngest man to win the American League batting crown?

41. Can you name the relief pitcher who set a big league record with 62 saves in 2008?

42. Which team tied a big league record with 116 wins in 2001?

43. Who holds the MLB single season record with 191 RBI in 1930?

44. Who is the catcher that holds the American League record for most no-hitters caught with four?

45. Which pitcher surrendered Roger Maris' then-record 61st home run in 1961?

46. Which Hall of Famer holds the record for most Gold Glove Awards as a shortstop?

47. Who holds the record for most career pinch hits?

48. Which player holds the record for most batting titles as a catcher with three?

49. At six feet, eleven inches, this former pitcher is the tallest player in major league history. Can you name him?

50. Which relief pitcher holds the record for most career appearances?

On September 19, 1998, Cal Ripken Jr. set the record for consecutive games played at 2,632.

Photo credit: Richard Lasner/National Baseball Hall of Fame and Museum

Answers

1. Eddie Gaedel, who measured three feet, seven inches, when he debuted with the St. Louis Browns in 1951.

2. Iván Rodríguez caught in 2,427 games with six different teams during his career.

3. Phil Niekro won 121 games after his fortieth birthday while playing for the Braves, Yankees, Indians, and Blue Jays.

4. Pitching for the Mets, Tom Seaver set the major league record for most consecutive strikeouts in a game with 10 versus the Padres on April 22, 1970. Over 50 years later, both Aaron Nola of the Phillies and Corbin Burnes of the Brewers duplicated the feat during the 2021 season.

5. Steve Garvey began his streak on September 3, 1975, and played 1,207 consecutive games with the Dodgers and Padres until it ended after the first game of a doubleheader on July 29, 1983.

6. Ken and Bob Forsch are the only brothers to have thrown no-hitters in the big leagues. Ken's came for the Astros (April 7, 1979), and Bob pitched a pair for the Cardinals (April 16, 1978, and September 26, 1983).

7. Playing outfield for the Cardinals, Vince Coleman stole at least 100 bases in each of his first three big league seasons from 1985–1987.

8. Rogers Hornsby holds the record for the highest career batting average by a right-handed batter, posting a .358 mark over his twenty-three-year major league career.

9. Jim Tobin of the Boston Braves tossed a 6-5 complete-game victory against the visiting Cubs, while also swatting three homers on May 13, 1942.

10. Fernando Tatís Jr. of the Cardinals hit two grand slams off Dodger pitcher Chan Ho Park in the third inning of their game on April 23, 1999.

11. Tony Gwynn, who finished with a lifetime .338 batting average, won a NL record-tying eight batting titles (1984, 1987–1989, 1994–1997).

12. Cal Ripken Jr. played in 2,632 consecutive games beginning on May 30, 1982, against the Blue Jays and ending after a September 19, 1998, game against the Yankees.

13. Keith Hernandez won eleven Gold Glove Awards during his seventeen-year big league career.

14. Owen Wilson hit 36 triples for the 1912 Pittsburgh Pirates. No other post-1900 player has hit more than 26 in a season.

15. Stan Musial hit six home runs and recorded three pinch hits during his 24 All-Star Game appearances.

16. George Sisler previously held the record, recording 257 hits with the St. Louis Browns in 1920.

17. Jack Morris recorded the most wins in the 1980s with 162, all with the Tigers.

18. Hank Aaron was selected to an incredible 25 All-Star teams in his career.

19. The Dodgers' Al Downing allowed Aaron's historic home run on April 8, 1974, at Atlanta-Fulton County Stadium.

20. In 1931, right fielder Earl Webb set the record for doubles in a season while playing for the Boston Red Sox.

21. On June 11, 1938, Johnny Vander Meer threw a no-hitter against the Boston Bees, and followed it up with another no-hitter in his next start against the Brooklyn Dodgers on June 15.

On April 22, 1970, Tom Seaver of the NY Mets became the first pitcher to strike out 10 consecutive batters.

Photo credit: National Baseball Hall of Fame and Museum

22. Eddie Cicotte, Red Faber, Dickey Kerr, and Lefty Williams of the 1920 White Sox each won at least 20 games, as did Mike Cuellar, Pat Dobson, Jim McNally, and Jim Palmer of the 1971 Orioles.

23. Tommy Brown was sixteen years, seven months, and twenty-eight days old when he started at shortstop for the Dodgers vs. the Cubs at Ebbets Field in 1944 during a manpower shortage due to World War II.

24. Satchel Paige, who was fifty-nine years, eighty days old when he pitched three innings for the Kansas City Athletics on September 25, 1965.

25. Moises Alou and Gary Sheffield; Alou represented the Expos, Marlins, Astros, Cubs, and Giants at All-Star Games, while Sheffield represented the Padres, Marlins, Dodgers, Braves, and Yankees.

26. Ty Cobb batted .366 over his twenty-four-year career with the Tigers and Athletics.

27. Mike Marshall made 106 appearances as a relief pitcher with the Dodgers in 1974.

28. Cubs first baseman Mark Grace had 1,754 total hits between 1990 and 1999.

29. Bill Wambsganss of the Cleveland Indians recorded an unassisted triple play against the Brooklyn Robins in the 1920 World Series.

30. Nolan Ryan struck out 383 batters in 1973, breaking the record for most strikeouts in a season held by the Dodgers Sandy Koufax.

31. The Athletics' Darold Knowles (1973) and the Dodgers' Brandon Morrow (2017) both appeared in all seven games of a World Series.

32. Brooks Robinson made 2,870 appearances at third base, all with the Orioles.

33. On September 16, 1975, Rennie Stennett of the Pirates batted lead-off and collected seven of his team's 24 hits in a 22-0 rout of the Cubs.

34. Charles "Old Hoss" Radbourn won an astounding 60 games for the Providence Grays in 1884, finishing the season with a 60-12 record and a 1.38 ERA.

35. Cal Ripken Jr. (Rochester) and Wade Boggs (Pawtucket), who both played third base for their respective teams.

36. Mark Lemke came to the plate 3,664 times in his big league career, the most of any player who was never hit by a pitch.

37. Deion Sanders played in the 1992 World Series with the Braves, and the 1994 and 1995 Super Bowls with the San Francisco 49ers and Dallas Cowboys, respectively.

38. John Wathan, who stole 36 bases for the Royals in 1982.

39. Tom Zachary went 12-0 for the Yankees in 1929, the most wins ever by a pitcher in a season where he was not charged with a loss. Two years earlier, in 1927, Zachary surrendered Babe Ruth's 60th home run of the season while he was pitching for the Senators.

40. In 1955, Tigers' outfielder Al Kaline, at age twenty, led the AL with a .340 batting average.

41. Angels closer Francisco Rodríguez set the major league record for saves in 2008 with 62.

42. The Seattle Mariners 116 wins tied the big league mark set by the NL's Chicago Cubs in 1906.

43. Cubs center fielder Hack Wilson set the single season record for RBI in 1930.

44. Jason Varitek caught no-hitters thrown by four different Red Sox pitchers: Hideo Nomo, Derek Lowe, Clay Buchholz, and Jon Lester.

45. Tracy Stallard of the Red Sox gave up Maris' record-breaking homer.

46. Former Padres and Cardinals shortstop Ozzie Smith won thirteen Gold Glove Awards during his nineteen-year big league career.

47. Lenny Harris recorded 212 pinch hits in 804 career pinch hit at-bats, both major league records.

48. Joe Mauer of the Twins, who won AL batting titles in 2006, 2008, and 2009.

49. Standing at a towering six feet, eleven inches, Jon Rauch was the tallest player in major league history.

50. Reliever Jesse Orosco, who appeared in 1,252 games during his twenty-four-year career with nine different franchises.

Rogers Hornsby holds the career record for batting average by a right-handed batter, with a .358 average.

Photo credit: Charles Conlon/National Baseball Hall of Fame and Museum

Chapter 6

Hall of Famers

"I hope someday that some of the young fellows coming into the game will know how it feels to be picked in the Hall of Fame."

—Babe Ruth during his Hall of Fame induction speech on June 12, 1939

1. Can you name the Hall of Famer who finished his career with 3,630 hits—getting exactly half (1,815) at home and half (1,815) on the road?

2. Whose 15th inning solo home run proved to be the winning margin in the 1967 All-Star Game?

3. Who holds the American League career mark for assists and putouts by an outfielder?

4. What future Hall of Famer became the first player to win a league MVP Award while playing for a team that finished in last place that season?

5. What manager has not only the most career wins in big league history, but also the most career losses?

6. Which Hall of Famer made his big league debut with the Padres without ever spending a day in the minors?

7. How many times did Hank Aaron, who finished his career with 755 home runs, hit at least 50 homers in a season?

8. With which team did Ryne Sandberg begin his big league career?

9. Who is the only player in history to lead his league in home runs for seven straight seasons?

10. Which future Hall of Famer won back-to-back National League Most Valuable Player Awards in 1975 and 1976?

11. What college did Hall of Fame third baseman Mike Schmidt attend?

12. Among players with at least 400 career stolen bases, which player owns the best success rate?

13. During the "Year of the Pitcher" in 1968, who was the only American League batter to post a batting average over .300?

14. Who is the only player in big league history to post seven consecutive seasons with at least a .300 batting average, 20 home runs, 100 RBI, 100 runs scored, and 100 walks?

15. Which future Hall of Famer was the Commissioner of Baseball in 1947 when Jackie Robinson broke the color barrier?

16. Which Hall of Famer holds the all-time record for highest career on-base percentage?

17. What is the name of the historic ballpark located in Cooperstown, New York?

18. Which Hall of Famer is the only Indians player to record at least 2,000 hits in a Cleveland uniform?

19. Which future Hall of Famer was named the unanimous NL MVP following the 1967 season?

20. With what club did Babe Ruth hit his 714th and final big league home run?

21. Which Hall of Fame pitcher holds the record for lowest postseason ERA?

22. After spending twenty-two seasons as a star outfielder with the Detroit Tigers, with what team did Hall of Famer Ty Cobb play his final two big league seasons of 1927 and 1928?

23. What 1954 Rule 5 Draft pick from the Dodgers organization went on to a Hall of Fame career with the Pirates?

24. Who was the last National League player to win the batting Triple Crown?

25. Who is the only skipper to be named the Baseball Writers' Association of America (BBWAA) Manager of the Year in two straight seasons?

26. Who is the only American League player to record at least 100 stolen bases in a season?

27. Who were the managers in the first All-Star Game in 1933?

28. Who is the all-time leader in games played among first basemen?

29. Who received the first Ford C. Frick Awards from the Baseball Hall of Fame in 1978 for broadcasting excellence?

30. Who are the only father and son combination inducted into the Hall of Fame?

31. Who is the only player to win a league MVP Award at both shortstop and center field?

32. Who is the only catcher to win back-to-back league Most Valuable Player Awards?

33. Who is the only player to win batting titles in three different decades?

34. Who is the only man to manage both the Brooklyn Dodgers and New York Yankees?

35. Who is the only player to win an American League batting title without hitting a home run?

36. Who led the 1959 Chicago White Sox, known as the "Go-Go Sox," with 56 stolen bases?

37. Which Hall of Famer holds the MLB career record with 792 doubles?

38. Which National Hockey League team drafted Hall of Fame pitcher Tom Glavine in the fourth round of the 1984 NHL Draft?

39. Who is the only Hall of Famer born in Idaho?

40. Which Hall of Famer won his 300th game with the SF Giants in 2009?

41. Willie Mays made "The Catch" in Game 1 of the 1954 World Series on a ball hit by which player?

42. Which Hall of Fame pitcher threw three shutouts in the 1905 World Series?

43. Which Hall of Famer began his career in the Negro Leagues with the Newark Eagles, before joining the NY Giants in 1949?

44. With what team did Paul Molitor collect his 3,000th hit?

45. What year were the first Hall of Fame elections held by the BBWAA?

46. Which pitcher struck out Babe Ruth, Lou Gehrig, Jimmie Foxx, Al Simmons, and Joe Cronin in succession during the 1934 All-Star Game?

47. In 1922, Detroit's Ty Cobb batted .401, but lost the American League batting title to whom?

48. What position did future Hall of Famer Jackie Robinson play when he debuted for the Brooklyn Dodgers in 1947?

49. When future Hall of Famer Lou Brock was traded to the Cardinals from the Cubs on June 15, 1964, which former National League 20-game winner did the Cubs receive in return?

50. Who was the last National League player to hit .400 in a season?

Stan Musial finished his career with 3,630 hits, with exactly half of his hits coming at home and the other half on the road.

Photo credit: National Baseball Hall of Fame and Museum

Answers

1. Stan Musial collected 3,630 hits during his twenty-two-year career with the Cardinals, with half of his hits coming at home and half on the road.

2. Tony Pérez won the game for the National League with his extra inning homer in the 1967 All-Star Game.

3. Hall of Famer Tris Speaker holds the AL career mark for assists (449) and putouts (6,788) by an outfielder.

4. Andre Dawson won the 1987 NL MVP Award with the last-place Cubs.

5. Connie Mack, in an amazing 53 seasons as a major league manager, finished with a career win-loss record of 3,731-3,948.

6. After playing at the University of Minnesota, outfielder Dave Winfield was selected by the Padres in the first round of the 1973 amateur draft. Without spending a day in the minors, he made his big league debut with the Padres on June 19, 1973.

7. Hank Aaron never hit 50 home runs in a season.

8. Ryne Sandberg played in 13 games with the Phillies in his debut season of 1981 before being traded to the Cubs, where he played his final 15 MLB seasons.

9. Ralph Kiner led the NL in home runs every year from 1946 through 1952.

Roberto Clemente began his pro career with the Montreal Royals in the Dodgers organization before joining the Pirates through the Rule 5 Draft.

Photo credit: National Baseball Hall of Fame and Museum

10. Cincinnati Reds second baseman Joe Morgan won back-to-back NL MVP Awards in 1975 and 1976.

11. Mike Schmidt played shortstop at Ohio University in Athens, Ohio.

12. Hall of Famer Tim Raines was successful on 84.7 percent of his stolen base attempts in his twenty-three-year big league career.

13. Carl Yastrzemski's .301 batting average in 1968 is the lowest ever for the winner of a batting title in the modern era.

14. Frank Thomas, a 2014 Hall of Fame inductee, set this unique mark in his first seven full seasons in the big leagues (1991-1997).

15. Happy Chandler was Commissioner when Jackie Robinson made his historic debut in 1947.

16. Ted Williams holds the record with a career on-base percentage of .482, reaching base in almost half of his career at-bats.

17. Doubleday Field, located just off Main Street in Cooperstown.

18. Napoleon Lajoie collected 2,047 hits playing for Cleveland from 1902 to 1914.

19. Cardinals' first baseman Orlando Cepeda won the NL MVP unanimously in 1967.

20. Ruth slugged his final home run with the Boston Braves.

21. Mariano Rivera holds the record with a 0.70 ERA over 141 postseason innings.

22. Ty Cobb finished his career with the Philadelphia Athletics.

23. Roberto Clemente played with the Montreal Royals, a Dodgers minor league affiliate, before being selected by the Pirates in the 1954 Rule 5 Draft.

24. Joe Medwick was the last player to win the NL Batting Triple Crown hitting .374, with 31 home runs and 154 RBI for the Cardinals in 1937.

25. Bobby Cox won back-to-back Manager of the Year Awards for the Braves in 2004 and 2005.

26. Rickey Henderson, who stole 100 bases in a season three times for the Athletics, set the modern-day record of 130 stolen bases in 1982.

27. In the first All-Star Game, Connie Mack managed the American League, with John McGraw managing the National League team.

28. Eddie Murray appeared in 2,413 games at first, more than any other player.

29. Legendary broadcasters Mel Allen and Red Barber were selected as the first Ford C. Frick Award winners.

30. Longtime baseball executive Larry MacPhail was inducted into the Hall of Fame in 1978. He was later joined by his son Lee, also an executive, who was inducted in 1998.

31. Robin Yount of the Brewers won the American League MVP as a shortstop in 1982 then won the award again in 1989 as a center fielder.

32. Yogi Berra won the AL MVP Award in both 1954 and 1955 following his first MVP in 1951.

33. George Brett won American League batting titles with the Royals in 1976, 1980, and 1990.

34. Casey Stengel managed the Dodgers from 1934–1936 and the Yankees from 1949–1960.

35. Rod Carew of the Twins led the Junior Circuit with a .318 batting average in 1972, though he did not homer the entire season.

36. Shortstop Luis Aparicio led both the White Sox and the AL in stolen bases in 1959.

37. Outfielder Tris Speaker set the career mark of 792 doubles over his twenty-two-year career.

38. The Los Angeles Kings selected Tom Glavine in the fourth round of 1984 NHL Draft, the same year the Braves drafted Glavine in the second round.

39. Harmon Killebrew, who was elected to the Hall of Fame in 1984, is the only Hall of Famer born in Idaho.

40. On June 4, 2009, Randy Johnson won his 300th game, defeating the Washington Nationals 5-1.

41. Mays made his famous over the shoulder catch on a ball hit by the Cleveland Indians' Vic Wertz.

42. Christy Mathewson tossed three shutouts in the New York Giants victory over the Philadelphia Athletics in the 1905 World Series.

43. Monte Irvin began his career in 1938 with the Newark Eagles of the Negro National League.

44. Molitor collected his 3,000th hit with the Minnesota Twins on September 16, 1996, against the KC Royals.

45. The first Hall of Fame elections were held in 1936, with the BBWAA electing Ty Cobb, Walter Johnson, Christy Mathewson, Babe Ruth, and Honus Wagner to the Hall of Fame.

46. NY Giants pitcher Carl Hubbell struck out the five future Hall of Famers in succession during the 1934 All-Star Game at the Polo Grounds.

47. Cobb lost the batting title to George Sisler, who hit an incredible .420 with the St. Louis Browns in 1922.

48. Jackie Robinson was the Dodgers regular first baseman in 1947 before moving to second base in 1948.

49. Former 20-game winner, Ernie Broglio, was traded to the Cubs along with Doug Clemens and Bobby Shantz for Lou Brock in 1964.

50. Bill Terry hit .401 for the 1930 Giants, the last player in the NL to accomplish the feat.

Ted Williams of the Red Sox holds the record with a career on-base percentage of .482.

Photo credit: National Baseball Hall of Fame and Museum

Chapter 7

Baseball in Pop Culture

"It breaks your heart. It is designed to break your heart. The game begins in the spring, when everything else begins again, and it blossoms in the summer, filling the afternoons and evenings, and then as soon as the chill rains come, it stops and leaves you to face the fall alone."

—A. Bartlett Giamatti, *The Green Fields of the Mind*

1. Can you name the former big leaguer who starred as the title character in the 1958–1963 television series *The Rifleman*?

2. Who was the historian who famously wrote the following in 1954: "Whoever wants to know the heart and mind of America had better learn baseball, the rules and realities of the game"?

3. A frustrated fan of what hopeless team makes a pact with the Devil to help the baseball team win the league pennant in the musical comedy *Damn Yankees*?

4. Who portrayed Oakland Athletics front office executive Billy Beane in the 2011 movie *Moneyball*?

5. Can you name the groundbreaking 1970 book written by former big league pitcher Jim Bouton chronicling his 1969 season with the Seattle Pilots and Houston Astros?

6. Who was the former catcher and longtime broadcaster who starred in the 1985–1990 television series *Mr. Belvedere*?

7. Who was the American League umpire from 1969 to 1979 who authored such humorous books as *The Umpire Strikes Back*, *Strike Two*, *The Fall of the Roman Empire*, *Remembrance of Swings Past*, and *Baseball Lite*?

8. Can you name the Broadway play about a baseball player coming out as gay during his playing career that won the 2003 Tony Award for Best Play?

9. Famously, Yankees' legend Mariano Rivera's walk-out song performed by Metallica was named what?

10. On the long-running TV hit *Seinfeld*, the character Elaine Benes was a fan of what big league team?

11. The 2002 film *The Rookie* ended with pitcher Jim Morris making his debut with what big league team at the age of thirty-five?

12. The 1989 comedy film *Major League* portrays the fictionalized version of what big league team?

13. The 1999 film *For Love of the Game* has actor Kevin Costner's aging character Billy Chapel tossing a perfect game for what big league team?

14. Can you name the Hall of Fame outfielder who famously appears in the 1988 comedy film *The Naked Gun?*

15. In the 1986 comedy *Ferris Bueller's Day Off*, Ferris attends a day game at what real-life big league ballpark?

16. "Candlesticks always make a nice gift" is a famous line from actor Robert Wuhl from what 1988 baseball comedy?

17. What actor famously says the line "There's no crying in baseball" in the 1992 film *A League of Their Own*?

18. What was the name of the minor league catcher Kevin Costner portrayed in *Bull Durham*?

19. In what year did the acclaimed television documentary miniseries *Baseball*, created by filmmaker Ken Burns, first air its original nine episodes?

20. Who wrote and performed the 1981 hit song "Talkin' Baseball (Willie, Mickey, and the Duke)"?

21. What song from Bruce Springsteen's 1984 hit album *Born in the USA* does the singer reference an encounter with a former baseball teammate?

22. Can you name the titular character in *The Natural*, an acclaimed book and movie in which a gifted pitcher returns to the game years later as a star outfielder and slugger?

23. Archibald "Moonlight" Graham, who famously appeared in the 1982 novel *Shoeless Joe*, on which the movie *Field of Dreams* was based, actually made a single 1905 major league appearance with what team?

24. Who wrote the 1966 baseball classic *The Glory of Their Times*, in which the author interviews more than two dozen players to get first-person accounts from the game's early years?

25. Actor James Earl Jones portrayed writer Terence Mann in what movie?

26. Can you name the two baseball films directed by Ron Shelton, a former minor league infielder in the Baltimore Orioles farm system from 1967 to 1971?

27. In *Who's on First?*, a routine made famous by comedy team Bud Abbott and Lou Costello, what is the pitcher's name?

28. Can you name the actor, comedian, and longtime fan of the New York Yankees who directed the 2001 HBO movie *61**?

29. The 1910 poem "Baseball's Sad Lexicon," written by Franklin Pierce Adams, references a famous infield made up of a trio of what Hall of Famers?

30. For what club did Casey play in the famous poem *Casey at the Bat*?

31. What was the first domed major league stadium?

32. Who is the author of the famed baseball book *The Boys of Summer*?

33. Future United States President George H.W. Bush played collegiate baseball for which university?

34. Which White Sox pitcher became the subject of a feature film starring Jimmy Stewart?

35. What actor portrayed Yankees' legend Lou Gehrig in the 1942 film *The Pride of the Yankees*?

36. What MLB team owner founded the All-American Girls Professional Baseball League in 1943?

37. Who starred as Jackie Robinson in the 1950 movie *The Jackie Robinson Story*?

38. Which artist wrote and performed the classic baseball song "Centerfield"?

39. What was the first year that the Topps Gum Company issued an all-baseball card set?

40. Who was the first major league player to be pictured on a United States postage stamp?

41. What is the famous nickname given to pitcher Mark Fidrych, who burst on the national scene with the Tigers in 1976 with 19 wins?

42. What team is associated with the menacing nickname "Murderers' Row"?

43. What 1979 World Series-winning team adopted the disco hit "We Are Family" as its theme song?

44. Who was the 1965 NL Rookie of the Year Award winner who later appeared on such TV shows as *Gilligan's Island* and *M*A*S*H*?

45. Who was the first athlete to appear on a Wheaties box?

46. What year did the video game *MLB: The Show* debut?

47. The made-for-television movie *It's Good to Be Alive* was based on the life of which Hall of Famer?

48. In 1970, Don Drysdale played himself in an episode of what popular television comedy series?

49. Which Hall of Famer had a candy bar name after them that was distributed to fans on opening day of the 1978 season?

50. What Hall of Fame shortstop was known as "The Wizard of Oz"?

Jackie Robinson was the first player featured on a US postage stamp in recognition of breaking baseball's color barrier in 1947.

Photo credit: National Baseball Hall of Fame and Museum

Answers

1. Chuck Connors, who played big league ball in parts of two seasons with the Dodgers (1949) and Cubs (1951).

2. The French American historian Jacques Barzun.

3. Middle-aged real estate agent Joe Boyd made a pact with the devil to help his favorite baseball team, the Washington Senators.

4. Brad Pitt, who was nominated for an Academy Award for his role as Billy Beane.

5. The controversial book *Ball Four* was released in 1970, providing readers with an insider's view of the game of baseball, both on and off the field.

6. Bob Uecker played sportswriter George Owens
    who employed the title character as the
    family butler.

7. Ron Luciano, who was known for his animated
    calls on the diamond, wrote five books filled
    with humorous anecdotes about his career as
    an umpire.

8. *Take Me Out*, written by playwright Richard
    Greenberg, tells the fictitious story of
    Darren Lemming who comes out as gay to
    his teammates.

9. Yankee closer Mariano Rivera took the
    mound at Yankee Stadium to Metallica's
    "Enter Sandman."

10. Elaine Benes was a fan of the Baltimore Orioles.

11. Jim Morris made his debut as a relief pitcher with the Tampa Bay Devil Rays.

12. The film portrays the Indians, who capped off their miraculous season by winning the AL East in a playoff game against the Yankees.

13. In his final game with the team Billy Chapel throws a perfect game for the Detroit Tigers against the Yankees.

14. Reggie Jackson played himself when he made his big screen debut in *The Naked Gun*.

15. Ferris Bueller plays "hooky" from school to attend a game at Chicago's Wrigley Field.

16. Robert Wuhl gave the famous line as manager Larry Hockett in the film *Bull Durham*.

17. Tom Hanks, who played former slugger and Rockford Peaches manager, Jimmy Dugan, in the movie.

18. Costner played minor league journeyman catcher Crash Davis.

19. The Emmy Award Winning documentary debuted on PBS in 1994.

20. Terry Cashman recorded the song for his album *Passin' It On: America's Baseball Heritage in Song*.

21. "Glory Days" references an encounter Springsteen had with a former high school teammate.

22. The *Natural* tells the story of Roy Hobbs and his mysterious baseball career.

23. "Moonlight" Graham played one inning in right field for the New York Giants in 1905.

24. *The Glory of Their Times* was written by Lawrence Ritter, who was a professor of economics and finance at New York University. Ritter authored a number of books on business and baseball.

When it opened in 1965, the Houston Astrodome became the first domed stadium in the majors.

Photo credit: National Baseball Hall of Fame and Museum

25. Jones played the reclusive writer Terence Mann in the 1989 film *Field of Dreams*.

26. Ron Shelton directed *Bull Durham* and *Cobb*.

27. Bud Abbott explains to an exasperated Lou Costello that his team's pitcher is named Tomorrow.

28. The made-for-television movie *61** was directed by Billy Crystal.

29. The Chicago Cubs infield of shortstop Joe Tinker, second baseman Johnny Evers, and first baseman Frank Chance, a group that helped the franchise win four NL championships and two World Series from 1906 to 1910.

30. Casey played for the Mudville nine.

31. When it opened in 1965, Houston's Astrodome was the first domed stadium in the majors.

32. *The Boys of Summer*, one of the most celebrated baseball books of all-time, was authored by Roger Kahn.

33. President George H.W. Bush played first base for the Yale baseball team from 1946-1948.

34. The *Stratton Story*, starring Jimmy Stewart as the title character, was based on the life of pitcher Monty Stratton, whose career was cut short by a tragic accident.

35. Gary Cooper played Lou Gehrig in *The Pride of the Yankees*, receiving an Academy Award nomination for Best Actor in a Leading Role.

36. Chewing gum mogul Philip Wrigley, who inherited the Chicago Cubs from his father, founded the AAGPBL in 1943.

37. Jackie Robinson played himself in this biopic.

38. Former Creedence Clearwater Revival frontman John Fogerty released *Centerfield* in 1985 on his solo album of the same name.

39. Topps first issued an all-baseball card set in 1951.

40. In 1982, Jackie Robinson became the first major league player to be pictured on a United States postage stamp.

41. Mark Fidrych was nicknamed "The Bird" because of his resemblance to the *Sesame Street* character "Big Bird."

42. "Murderers' Row" was the nickname given to the Yankees team of the late 1920s, often describing the first six hitters in the 1927 lineup: Earle Combs, Mark Koenig, Babe Ruth, Lou Gehrig, Bob Meusel, and Tony Lazzeri.

43. The Pittsburgh Pirates, who defeated the Baltimore Orioles in seven games to win the 1979 World Series.

44. Dodger infielder Jim Lefebvre, who was an actor in the off-season and after his retirement from baseball.

45. Lou Gehrig was the first athlete to appear on a Wheaties box in 1934.

46. *MLB: The Show* was first released by Sony in 2006.

47. The movie was based on the life of Dodger catcher Roy Campanella.

48. Don Drysdale appeared in an episode of *The Brady Bunch* in 1970.

49. The Reggie Bar was a round candy bar made of peanuts, caramel, and chocolate named after Reggie Jackson. It was given to fans who attended opening day at Yankee Stadium in 1978.

50. The St. Louis Cardinals Ozzie Smith, who was given the name for his defensive wizardry.

Reggie Jackson made his acting debut playing himself in the 1988 film *The Naked Gun*.

Photo credit: National Baseball Hall of Fame and Museum

Chapter 8

The Postseason

"Touch 'em all Joe! You'll never hit a bigger home run in your life!"

—Blue Jays broadcaster Tom Cheek after Joe Carter's 1993 World Series-winning HR

1. The New York Yankees have captured the most World Series titles with 27. What team has won the second most?

2. Who was the first player to win World Series MVPs for two different teams?

3. Which Milwaukee Braves pitcher won three games in the 1957 World Series?

4. Who holds the record for most World Series games played in history?

5. Who earned the nickname "Home Run" after hitting two home runs in the 1911 World Series?

6. Which three players share the record for most hits in a single World Series with 13?

7. Who are the only brothers to hit home runs in the same World Series?

8. In what year did an earthquake interrupt the World Series?

9. In what year was the first November World Series game played?

10. Which Hall of Famer holds the record for most home runs in World Series play with 18?

11. In what season did the Brooklyn Dodgers win their lone World Series title?

12. Who is the only player to steal at least seven bases in one World Series?

13. In what year did the Cubs and White Sox play in the only all-Chicago World Series?

14. What New York Giants player had three pinch hits and drove in seven runs in just six at-bats during the 1954 World Series?

15. Which Dodgers pinch hitter struck out to end Don Larsen's perfect game for the Yankees in the 1956 World Series?

16. Whose 13th inning home run won Game 1 of the 1995 ALDS against the Red Sox, giving the Indians their first postseason victory in forty-seven years?

17. What team won the first modern World Series in 1903?

18. What Dodgers pitcher was the first winner of the World Series MVP Award in 1955?

19. Which team won three straight World Series titles from 1972 to 1974?

20. What two teams went from last place in 1990 to first place 1991 and played in that season's World Series?

21. Who was the first Latin American manager to lead his team to a World Series title?

22. Which three Los Angeles Dodgers players shared the 1981 World Series MVP Award?

23. Who are the only two batters to end a World Series with a home run?

24. Which Dodgers pitcher won two games and saved two others in the 1959 World Series?

25. Which team set a record by sweeping three straight American League Championship Series from 1969-1971?

26. Who was the winning pitcher for the Mets in their famous Game 6 victory over the Red Sox in the 1986 World Series?

27. Which Hall of Fame pitcher holds the record for most World Series victories with 10?

28. Which Reds pitcher surrendered Carlton Fisk's legendary Game 6 home run in the 1975 World Series?

29. Which Hall of Fame pitcher won two games in the 1948 World Series with the Indians, then managed the Yankees to the 1978 World Series crown?

30. Which Yankees player was named the MVP of the 1960 World Series despite playing on the losing team?

31. Who was the only player to end a World Series by being caught stealing?

32. Which Indians pitcher was credited with the victory in the team's one-game playoff against the Red Sox in 1948?

33. What was the first year the modern World Series was decided in the seventh-and-final game?

34. Who was the only pitcher to have thrown a no-hitter in the regular season and in the postseason?

35. Which manager led the Red Sox to their first World Series title in eighty-six years in 2004?

36. Who is the only pitcher to win a World Series game in three decades?

37. Which Hall of Famer is known for his "Mad Dash" in Game 7 of the 1946 World Series?

38. Who is the only player to win MVP of the regular season, LCS, and World Series in the same year?

39. Who was the first manager to win a World Series in both the AL and the NL?

40. Who was on base in Game 3 of the 1951 NL playoff when Bobby Thomson hit his pennant-winning home run for the Giants?

41. What pitcher threw a 10-inning shutout in Game 7 of the 1991 World Series to lead the Twins to the title over the Braves?

42. Which teams played in the first American League and National League Championship Series in 1969?

43. Who was on the mound for the final out of the 1969 World Series?

44. Which pitcher did Kirk Gibson hit his dramatic pinch-hit walk-off home run in Game 1 of the 1988 World Series?

45. Name the four players who've homered three times in a World Series game?

46. In 1978, the Yankees Bucky Dent homered off which Boston Red Sox pitcher in their dramatic tie-breaker game to determine the AL East winner?

47. In 1961 Whitey Ford set the record for consecutive scoreless innings pitched in the World Series, breaking the record held by which pitcher?

48. From 1932 through 1947, the Yankees won eight World Series titles. What was the only other American League team to win the World Series in that span?

49. In what year did the Cardinals and Browns meet in the only all-St. Louis World Series?

50. Who was the last manager in Indians history to lead the team to a World Series title?

The Mets celebrate after their dramatic defeat of the Red Sox in the 1986 World Series.

Photo credit: Tom Heitz/National Baseball Hall of Fame and Museum

Answers

1. The St. Louis Cardinals, who've won 11 World Series titles.

2. Reggie Jackson, with the Oakland Athletics in 1973 and Yankees in 1977.

3. In 1957, Lew Burdette helped the Braves defeat the Yankees in seven games, the franchise's only World Series victory while in Milwaukee.

4. Yogi Berra appeared in 14 World Series with the Yankees, playing in 75 games.

5. John Franklin "Home Run" Baker of the Philadelphia Athletics was given his nickname after hitting a home run in Games 2 and 3 of the 1911 World Series against the Giants.

6.   Bobby Richardson of the Yankees in 1964,
     Lou Brock of the Cardinals in 1968, and Marty
     Barrett of the Red Sox in 1986.

7.   Ken and Clete Boyer are the only brothers
     to hit home runs in the same World Series,
     both connecting in Game 7 of the 1964 Fall
     Classic: Ken for the Cardinals and Clete for
     the Yankees.

8.   The 1989 World Series was played between
     the Oakland Athletics and the San Francisco
     Giants. On October 17, just minutes before the
     start of Game 3, a magnitude 6.9 earthquake
     struck the Bay Area, causing significant
     damage to both Oakland and San Francisco.
     The series resumed on October 27.

9. The tragic attacks of 9/11 pushed back the start of the 2001 postseason. As a result, Game 4 of the World Series between the Yankees and Diamondbacks, which started on October 31, but ended after midnight, became the first World Series game played in November.

10. Mickey Mantle slugged 18 home runs in 12 World Series appearances with the Yankees.

11. The Dodgers defeated the Yankees in the 1955 World Series to win their first and only title in Brooklyn.

12. Lou Brock, who stole seven bases in both the 1967 and 1968 World Series.

Yogi Berra of the NY Yankees played in more World Series games than any other player, appearing in 75 games across 14 World Series.

Photo credit: National Baseball Hall of Fame and Museum

13. The White Sox defeated the Cubs, four games to two, in the 1906 World Series.

14. Dusty Rhodes batted .667 to help lead the Giants past the Indians in the 1954 World Series.

15. Dale Mitchell struck out ending Game 5 in which the Yankees defeated the Dodgers 2-0.

16. Tony Peña homered off Zane Smith of the Red Sox in the bottom of the 13th inning to win the game for the Indians.

17. The Boston Americans defeated the Pittsburgh Pirates in a best-of-nine series, five games to three, to win the first World Series.

18. Johnny Podres was selected the series MVP after tossing a complete-game shutout against the Yankees in Game 7 of the 1955 World Series.

19. The Oakland Athletics defeated the Reds (1972), Mets (1973), and Dodgers (1974) in three consecutive World Series.

20. In 1991, the Minnesota Twins and Atlanta Braves won their respective divisions and met in the World Series after finishing in the last place the previous season.

21. Venezuelan-born Ozzie Guillén led the Chicago White Sox to the title in 2005.

22. Ron Cey, Pedro Guerrero, and Steve Yeager
shared the MVP Award after the Dodgers'
victory over the Yankees in the 1981
World Series.

23. The Pirates' Bill Mazeroski (1960) and Blue Jays'
Joe Carter (1993) are the only batters to hit
walk-off series clinching home runs for their
teams in the World Series.

24. Larry Sherry outshined future Hall of Famers
Don Drysdale and Sandy Koufax in the Dodgers'
victory over the White Sox.

25. The Baltimore Orioles swept the Twins in both
1969 and 1970 and the Oakland A's in 1971.

26. Rick Aguilera pitched the final two innings, picking up the win for the Mets.

27. Whitey Ford earned ten wins while pitching in eleven World Series with the Yankees.

28. Carlton Fisk homered off Pat Darcy in the bottom of the 12th inning, leading the Red Sox to victory in Game 6 of the series.

29. Bob Lemon won Game 2 and Game 6 of the 1948 World Series. Later in his career, he led the Yankees to their second consecutive title in 1978.

30. Bobby Richardson hit .367 and drove in a record 12 runs in New York's seven-game loss to the Pirates.

31. Babe Ruth was thrown out stealing in the ninth inning of Game 7 of the 1926 World Series by Cardinals catcher Bob O'Farrell.

32. Gene Bearden pitched a complete game, winning 8-3 over the Red Sox for his 20th win of the season.

33. 1909, when the Pirates defeated the Tigers for their first title.

34. In 2010, Roy Halladay of the Phillies pitched a perfect game against the Marlins in the regular season, and then tossed a no-hitter against the Reds in the first game of the NLDS.

35. In 2004, Terry Francona led the Red Sox their first World Series title since 1918.

36. Baltimore's Jim Palmer is the only pitcher to win a World Series game in three decades (1966, 1970, 1971, and 1983).

37. Enos Slaughter scored from first base on a hit by Harry Walker in the bottom of the eighth inning to lift the Cardinals to a 4-3 win over the Red Sox.

38. Future Hall of Famer Willie Stargell accomplished the feat in 1979 with the Pirates.

39. Sparky Anderson won back-to-back World Series with the Reds in 1975 and 1976, and later won a title with the Detroit Tigers in 1984.

40. Clint Hartung was on third after entering the game as a pinch runner for Don Mueller, and Whitey Lockman was on second after hitting a double to drive in a run.

41. Jack Morris pitched the complete-game shutout, winning the World Series MVP.

42. The Orioles triumphed over the Twins in the AL series, and the Mets defeated the Braves in the NL.

43. Jerry Koosman pitched a complete game in the NY Mets 5-3 victory over the Baltimore Orioles in the final game of the 1969 World Series.

44. Gibson homered off future Hall of Famer Dennis Eckersley with two outs in the bottom of the ninth inning.

45. Babe Ruth (1926 and 1928), Reggie Jackson (1977), Albert Pujols (2011), and Pablo Sandoval (2012) are the only players to homer three times in any World Series game.

46. Dent homered off Red Sox starter Mike Torrez in the top of seventh inning giving the Yankees a 3-2 lead. The Yankees would go on to defeat the Red Sox 5-4.

47. Ford pitched 33 2/3 consecutive scoreless innings across the 1960 and 1961 World Series, breaking Babe Ruth's record of 29 2/3 innings set while pitching for the Red Sox.

48. Detroit Tigers, with wins in 1935 and 1945.

49. The Cardinals defeated the Browns four games to two to win the 1944 World Series.

50. Lou Boudreau led the Indians to a World Series victory over the Boston Braves in 1948.

Dodgers fans take to the streets to celebrate their team's victory in the 1955 World Series.

Photo credit: National Baseball Hall of Fame and Museum

Chapter 9

Baseball Potpourri

"I made a major contribution to the Cardinals' pennant drive in 1964. I got hepatitis."

—Former player, current broadcaster, and funnyman Bob Uecker

1. Who was the last player/manager in the American League?

2. What former Michigan State track star was hired by the Oakland Athletics as a pinch-runner specialist, playing in 105 big league games without ever coming to bat?

3. What is the full name of Cal McLish, a big league pitcher for 15 seasons between 1944 and 1964?

4. Who are the only pair of brothers to have each won a major league batting title?

5. Who is the only pitcher to surrender more than 10 home runs in a season in which he saved 50 or more games?

6. Who is the only pitcher to record a victory in the All-Star Game without retiring a batter?

7. What two players tied for the 1979 National League Most Valuable Player Award?

8. Who is the only player in major league history to record 500 hits with four different teams?

9. Who was the only person to play big league ball across the 1940s, 1950s, 1960s, 1970s, and 1980s?

10. Who are the only two pitchers to record 10 or more shutouts in a season since the pitcher's mound height was lowered to 12 inches in 1969?

11. What is the mathematical formula for fielding average?

12. Who is the only member of the 3,000-Hit Club with fewer than 50 career home runs?

13. What is the maximum number of hits a team can make in one inning without scoring a run?

14. Who is the only player to win back-to-back Most Valuable Player Awards with two different clubs?

15. Who are the only two pitchers since World War II to win at least 20 games and lose at least 20 games in the same season?

16. In 2007, two players hit 20 or more doubles, triples, and home runs. For good measure, they both stole over 20 bases. Who were they?

17. Which future Hall of Famer played center field for the Cleveland Indians when future Hall of Fame pitcher Bob Feller no-hit the Yankees on April 30, 1946?

18. Which Hall of Famer was drafted by four professional sports leagues?

19. Who are the only two Heisman Trophy winners who went on to play major league baseball?

20. How many stitches are in a regulation MLB baseball?

21. Which former pitcher is the brother of tennis great Billie Jean King?

22. According to the Official Rules of Baseball, any fielder may wear a glove, but only two positions are allowed to wear a mitt. Which positions are they?

23. What member of the 1957 World Series champion Milwaukee Braves was also a member of the 1958–1959, 1959–1960 and 1960–1961 NBA champion Boston Celtics?

24. What was the last season in which both the National League and American League MVP Award went to pitchers?

25. Who was the only player to participate in a regular season perfect game and a World Series perfect game?

26. In inches, how wide is home plate?

27. What former punter for the 1994 National Champion Nebraska Cornhuskers football team was the only player to win Gold Gloves as an infielder and outfielder?

28. Who holds the distinction of being the 3,000th strikeout victim of both Nolan Ryan and Bob Gibson?

29. Who was the only member of the Seattle Pilots to lead the league in a major offensive category?

30. How many bases are awarded to the batter if a fielder deliberately touches a fair ball with his cap?

31. Can you name the catcher who caught no-hitters thrown by both Sandy Koufax and Nolan Ryan?

32. Which managers were traded for each other on August 3, 1960?

33. From 1960 through 1974, Maury Wills or Lou Brock led the National League in stolen bases in every year except one. Who led the NL in steals in 1970 to interrupt the fifteen-year dominance of Wills and Brock?

34. Which defensive player on the diamond is the only one allowed to start play in foul territory?

35. Who is the only player to win back-to-back All-Star Game MVP Awards?

36. Miguel Cabrera is one of two players to win at least four batting titles but is not a Hall of Famer. Can you name the other player?

37. Since 1950, who is the only player to win a league MVP Award but never be named to an All-Star Game during his career?

38. Which Olympic gold medalist later played major league baseball with the New York Giants?

39. What big league team moved to Baltimore to become the Orioles in 1954?

40. What two expansion teams joined the National League in 1962?

41. What native of Cuba pitched the first game for the expansion Seattle Pilots in 1969 and the first game for the expansion Seattle Mariners in 1977?

42. On April 13, 1980, the Kansas City Royals became the first team in major league history to feature a battery with two players who had last names beginning with the letter "Q." Can you name this pitcher and catcher?

43. In what years did the New York Yankees and New York Mets share Shea Stadium as their home park?

44. What Negro Leagues team did Hank Aaron play for before signing with the Boston Braves?

45. Who is the only woman member of the Baseball Hall of Fame?

46. Which Hall of Famer was known as the "Flying Dutchman"?

47. What is the oldest ballpark in the major leagues?

48. Who is the only player to have appeared in games for the Boston Braves, the Milwaukee Braves, and the Atlanta Braves?

49. Who are the only brothers to have posted major league hitting streaks of 30 or more games?

50. In 1973, who became baseball's first designated hitter?

Dave Winfield was drafted by teams in four professional sports leagues - MLB, NFL, NBA and ABA.

Photo credit: National Baseball Hall of Fame and Museum

Answers

1. Don Kessinger managed the White Sox as an active player in 1979. He resigned midway through the season and was replaced with future Hall of Fame manager Tony La Russa.

2. Herb Washington played for the Athletics solely as a pinch runner during the 1974 and 1975 seasons.

3. Calvin Coolidge Julius Caesar Tuskahoma McLish.

4. Dixie Walker (1944 NL champion at .357) and Harry Walker (1947 NL champion at .363).

5. Rod Beck, who saved 51 games in 1998, while allowing 11 home runs.

6. Dean Stone of the Senators entered the 1954 All-Star Game with runners on first and third and two outs in the top of the eighth inning, with the AL trailing 9-8. Stone immediately got out of the jam when Red Schoendienst of the Cardinals was caught stealing home. The AL scored three runs in the bottom of the eighth to take an 11-9 lead, and Virgil Trucks relieved Stone to start the ninth and wrapped up the AL's win.

7. The Cardinals Keith Hernandez and the Pirates Willie Stargell.

8. Rusty Staub had 500 hits for the Astros, Expos, Mets, and Tigers.

9. Minnie Miñoso, who played in 1949, 1951–1964, 1976, and 1980.

10. The Orioles Jim Palmer, who tossed 10 shutouts in 1975, and the Cardinals John Tudor, who had 10 shutouts in 1985.

11. Divide the sum of a fielder's putouts and assists by the sum of putouts, assists, and errors.

12. Infielder Eddie Collins had 3,315 career hits, with only 47 home runs.

13. Six (three singles load the bases, runners on second and third are picked off, two more singles load the bases again, final single hits a runner for an automatic hit and third out of the inning).

14. Barry Bonds, who won the National League MVP in 1992 with Pirates and 1993 with the Giants.

15. The White Sox Wilbur Wood, who went 24-20 in 1973, and the Atlanta Braves' Phil Niekro, who had a 21-20 record in 1979.

16. The Tigers' Curtis Granderson, and Jimmy Rollins of the Phillies.

17. Rookie Bob Lemon played center field for the Indians, going 1-for-4 in Feller's 1-0 no-hit victory over the Yankees.

18. Dave Winfield was drafted by teams in four professional sports leagues (MLB, NFL, NBA, and ABA).

19. 1950 Heisman winner Vic Janowicz played in MLB from 1953–1954, and Bo Jackson, who won the award in 1985, played in MLB from 1986–1991 and 1993–1994.

20. There are 108 stitches in the leather of each regulation MLB baseball.

21. Reliever Randy Moffitt, who had a twelve-year career in the majors pitching for the Giants, Astros, and Blue Jays.

22. The first baseman and catcher are allowed to wear a mitt.

23. Gene Conley, who stood at six feet, eight inches, pitched for the Braves and played power forward for the Celtics.

24. In 1968, when Bob Gibson won the NL MVP Award and Denny McLain won the award in the AL.

25. Jim Gilliam, who played for Brooklyn during Don Larsen's 1956 World Series perfect game and for Los Angeles during Sandy Koufax's masterpiece of 1965.

26. Home plate measures 17 inches across.

27. The Angels Darin Erstad won Gold Gloves as an outfielder in 2000 and 2002, and as a first baseman in 2004.

28. While an outfielder with the Reds, César Gerónimo was the 3,000th strikeout of both Nolan Ryan (July 4, 1980) and Bob Gibson (July 17, 1974).

Minnie Miñoso is the only player to have played in the majors during the 1940s, 1950s, 1960s, 1970s and 1980s.

Photo credit: National Baseball Hall of Fame and Museum

29. Tommy Harper led the American League with 73 stolen bases in 1969, the only season the Pilots played in the American League. In 1970, the Pilots moved to Milwaukee to become the Brewers.

30. The batter is awarded three bases if a fielder deliberately touches a fair ball with his cap.

31. Jeff Torborg caught Sandy Koufax's perfect game in 1965 and Nolan Ryan's first no-hitter in 1973.

32. Indians' manager Joe Gordon was traded for the Tigers' skipper Jimmy Dykes.

33. Bobby Tolan led the NL with 57 stolen bases for the Cincinnati Reds in 1970.

34. The catcher is the only defender allowed to start play in foul territory.

35. Mike Trout was named the MVP of the All-Star Game in both 2014 and 2015.

36. Bill Madlock, who won National League batting titles in 1975, 1976, 1981, and 1983.

37. Kirk Gibson was named the 1988 National League MVP with the Dodgers but was never an All-Star during his seventeen-year big league career.

38. Jim Thorpe, who won the pentathlon and decathlon during the 1912 Summer Olympics, joined the Giants in 1913 as a part-time outfielder.

39. After playing in St. Louis from 1902–1953, the Browns moved to Baltimore in 1954 and were renamed the Orioles.

40. New York Mets and Houston Colt .45's joined the NL in 1962.

41. Diego Seguí pitched in relief for the Pilots and started for the Mariners.

42. Reliever Dan Quisenberry pitched 2 1/3 innings in the Royals 3-2 victory over the Tigers. His battery-mate was catcher Jamie Quirk.

43. The Yankees and Mets shared Shea Stadium during the 1974–1975 seasons when Yankee Stadium went through an extensive renovation.

44. Hank Aaron played briefly for the Indianapolis Clowns of the Negro American League in 1952 before he was acquired by the Braves.

45. Effa Manley, who was elected to the Hall of Fame in 2006, was the general manager of the Negro National League's Newark Eagles.

46. Honus Wagner was given the moniker due to his German heritage and speed on the base paths.

47. Boston's Fenway Park, the home of the Red Sox since it opened in 1912, is the oldest ballpark in the major leagues.

48. Eddie Mathews began his career with the Boston Braves in 1952 and played for the team when the franchise moved to Milwaukee and later Atlanta.

49. Joe DiMaggio (56-game streak in 1941) and Dom DiMaggio (34-game streak in 1949).

50. Ron Blomberg of the Yankees became the AL's first designated hitter in a game against the Red Sox on April 6, 1973, at Fenway Park.

Eddie Mathews is the only player in Braves franchise history to play for the team in Boston, Milwaukee and Atlanta.

Photo credit: National Baseball Hall of Fame and Museum

Hall-of-Famer-signed baseballs from the Hall of Fame collection.

Photo credit: Milo Stewart Jr./National Baseball Hall of Fame and Museum

Acknowledgements

Thank you to the staff of the National Baseball Hall of Fame and Museum, with special thanks to the following individuals for their help in researching, writing, editing, and preparing the trivia questions, quotes, and photographs included in this book: Kelli Bogan, Bill Francis, Sean Gahagan, John Horne, Cassidy Lent, Scot Mondore, and Craig Muder.

In addition, we thank Jane Kinney Denning, Elina Diaz, Brenda Knight, Lisa McGuinness, Chris McKenney, and Robin Miller of Mango Publishing, and our agent, Valerie Tomaselli of MTM Publishing.

Finally, and certainly not least, we thank the good folks at Baseball-Reference.com, Retrosheet.org and SABR for their dedication and diligence in maintaining baseball's historical statistics, box scores, and biographical information. Each was an invaluable resource in developing this book.

Baseball's legends are immortalized in bronze in the Baseball Hall of Fame Plaque Gallery.

Photo credit: Milo Stewart Jr./National Baseball Hall of Fame and Museum

About the National Baseball Hall of Fame and Museum

The National Baseball Hall of Fame and Museum is an independent not-for-profit educational institution, dedicated to fostering an appreciation of the historical development of baseball and its impact on our culture by collecting, preserving, exhibiting, and interpreting its collections for a global audience as well as honoring those who have made outstanding contributions to our National Pastime. Opening its doors for the first time on June 12, 1939, the Hall of Fame has stood as the definitive repository of the game's treasures and as a symbol of the most profound individual honor bestowed on an athlete. It is every fan's "Field of Dreams," with its stories, legends, and magic shared from generation to generation.

Visit baseballhall.org and follow us on @BaseballHall on Twitter, Facebook, and Instagram for all the latest Hall of Fame news and fascinating stories from the National Pastime.

Mango Publishing, established in 2014, publishes an eclectic list of books by diverse authors—both new and established voices—on topics ranging from business, personal growth, women's empowerment, LGBTQ studies, health, and spirituality to history, popular culture, time management, decluttering, lifestyle, mental wellness, aging, and sustainable living. We were recently named 2019 *and* 2020's #1 fastest-growing independent publisher by *Publishers Weekly*. Our success is driven by our main goal, which is to publish high-quality books that will entertain readers as well as make a positive difference in their lives.

Our readers are our most important resource; we value your input, suggestions, and ideas. We'd love to hear from you—after all, we are publishing books for you!

Please stay in touch with us and follow us at:

Facebook: Mango Publishing
Twitter: @MangoPublishing
Instagram: @MangoPublishing
LinkedIn: Mango Publishing
Pinterest: Mango Publishing
Newsletter: mangopublishinggroup.com/newsletter

Join us on Mango's journey to reinvent publishing, one book at a time.